Vocational A-lev
Hospitality and Catering

Mary Aslett
Richard Gower

Pearson Education Limited
Edinburgh Gate
Harlow
Essex CM20 2JE
England

and Associated Companies throughout the world
Visit us on the World Wide Web at:
http://www.pearsoneduc.com

ISBN 0 582 36865 0

British Library Cataloguing-in-Publication Data

A catalogue record for this book is available from the British Library.

Set by 35 in Humanist, Rotis Serif, Caslon
Printed by Henry Ling Ltd at the Dorset Press, Dorchester, Dorset, DT1 1HD

10 9 8 7 6 5 4 3
05 04 03 02 01

Contents

		Page number
Introduction		v
Acknowledgements		x
UNIT 1	**An introduction to the hospitality and catering industry**	**1**
	The scale and scope of hospitality and catering nationally	3
	The structure of the hospitality and catering industry	5
	Employment	13
	External influences on the hospitality and catering industry	17
	Internal influences on the hospitality and catering industry	20
	Investigating and using information sources	22
	Revision questions	25
	Unit 1 key skills	28
UNIT 2	**Food and drink operations**	**31**
	Evaluating food and drink operations	33
	Food preparation and cooking	36
	Food and drink service	50
	Revision questions	67
	Unit 2 key skills	68
UNIT 3	**Accommodation and front office**	**71**
	Accommodation services	73
	Front office services	97
	Legal requirements	134
	Revision questions	141
	Unit 3 key skills	142

UNIT 4   **Customer service**   **145**

Providing excellent customer service   147
Understanding quality customer service standards   153
Programme evaluation in practice   158
Good and bad customer service   164
Revision questions   165
Unit 4 key skills   166

UNIT 5   **Safety, security and the environment**   **169**

Maintaining safety, security and environmental protection   171
Safety in the workplace   173
Good practice for ensuring safety, security and environmental
protection   175
Legislation   183
Food hygiene and safety   196
Security in hospitality and catering   203
Protecting the environment   205
Supervising, monitoring and managing safety, security and
the environment   209
Information sources   211
Revision questions   213
Unit 5 key skills   214

UNIT 6   **Purchasing, costing and control**   **217**

Purchasing and control in outlets   219
Calculating the selling price   230
Storage and issuing   238
Presentation and use of data and information   242
Revision questions   245
Unit 6 key skills   247

Appendix: Drink compendium   **251**

Index   **259**

Introduction

This book will assist tutors and students with the new Vocational A-level mandatory units in Hospitality and Catering. A full explanation of course assessment is given below:

The Vocational A-level full award is made up of 12 units.
The Vocational A-level single award is made up of six units.

Full award

Compulsory units

Unit 1 – The Hospitality and Catering Industry

In this unit you will gain an understanding of the scale and scope of the hospitality and catering industry by investigating organizations and outlets in different sectors of the industry.

This unit is assessed externally.

Unit 2 – Food and Drink Operations

In this unit you will gain an understanding of food and drink operations within hospitality and catering outlets and the range of staff who work in these areas. You will also investigate and observe preparing, cooking and service systems and learn how to evaluate their effectiveness.

This unit is assessed through your portfolio.

Unit 3 – Accommodation and Front Office Operations

In this unit you will explore the role of accommodation and front office operations within different types of outlets. You will research, compare and evaluate different outlets providing accommodation and front office services.

This unit is assessed through your portfolio.

Unit 4 – Customer Service

In this unit you will study the provision of customer service in hospitality and catering outlets. You will look at the procedures and practices used by supervisors to maintain and improve the standards of quality customer service.

This unit is assessed through your portfolio.

Unit 5 – Safety, Security and the Environment

In this unit you will learn how safety, security and the environment are managed in hospitality and catering outlets.

This unit is assessed externally.

Unit 6 – Purchasing, Costing and Control

In this unit you will study purchasing, costing and control in the daily operations of hospitality and catering outlets.

This unit is assessed through your portfolio.

Optional units

Each awarding body has its own set of optional units. You must complete six optional units, at least two of which must be assessed externally.

Assessment

At least one-third of your course will be externally assessed through tests, set projects or assignments, or case study work. The remainder will be assessed in your school or college through a programme of assignments set and marked by your teachers or lecturers.

Single award

The single award comprises six units, at least two of which must be externally assessed.

Key Skills

As well as covering the hospitality and catering units, you will also be able to develop your key skills in the areas of:

- ✪ **communication**
- ✪ **application of number**
- ✪ **information technology**
- ✪ **problem solving**
- ✪ **working with others**
- ✪ **improving own learning and performance**

While you are working on your hospitality and catering units, you will have the opportunity to develop and collect evidence for these key skills, although you will not necessarily cover every aspect. Other opportunities may arise through your lessons, individual studies and work experience.

The portfolio

You will need to compile a portfolio of evidence in order to achieve your Vocational A-level. Many of the ideas, tables, self-check lists and charts already presented in the mandatory units will be directly relevant to the portfolio.

What is a portfolio?

A portfolio collects together all the evidence you are submitting to show that you have fulfilled the Vocational A-level standards, including the criteria for the mandatory and optional units and usually the key skills units. As it will represent one or two years' work and will probably contain many types of evidence (see below), it is likely that you will want to use a lever arch file and maybe a box file.

What will a portfolio contain?

Your portfolio is likely to contain a variety of evidence:

- ✪ **assignments**
- ✪ **reports**
- ✪ **projects**
- ✪ **essays**
- ✪ **case studies**
- ✪ **letters**

- **memos**
- **artefacts produced by you**
- **work experience diary**
- **peer group assessments**
- **self assessments**
- **reports of assessments of simulation or role play exercises**
- **photographs**
- **audio and video recordings**
- **internal tests**

During your programme, you may also be assessed by observation or oral questioning. Your portfolio will contain evidence of the assessments carried out and, where appropriate, details of your own planning and evaluation of these activities.

As part of your programme you will visit establishments who provide specialist services which are complementary to the programme you are following. These may include some of the following:

- **a fish market**
- **a meat market**
- **a hotel**
- **an industrial catering unit**
- **a cook–chill unit**
- **a specialist food shop**
- **a hospital**
- **a university hall of residence**
- **a fast food outlet**

Visits are a good way to see how the knowledge and skills which you have acquired are actually put into practice. They will provide you with the opportunity to talk to practising specialists about the work they do. They may also provide you with useful facts, information and evidence of various kinds to use and display in your portfolio.

Presentation and record keeping

As your portfolio will contain a large amount of material, it is essential that it is well organized. An assessor or verifier should be able to see clearly how the evidence within the portfolio relates to the units.

The task of organizing the portfolio is made easier by accurate record keeping. You will probably be provided with a set of documents which may include:

- **a portfolio front or cover sheet stating your name, the name of your school or college and the name of the qualification**
- **a contents sheet listing the assignments, assessments and other forms of evidence included in your portfolio – you may give each piece of evidence a code number, to facilitate cross-referencing**
- **a summary record sheet indicating the units that have been completed**
- **a cover sheet for each activity (including assignments) that you have undertaken, listing such details as the date of completion and the task set**
- **an activity assessment sheet on which assessors and verifiers record their comments**
- **a grading record sheet to keep a record of the grades you have achieved**

Don't worry if you find all this paperwork hard to come to terms with at first – once you have completed a few assignments and become familiar with the procedures, it should begin to make more sense.

Who marks the assessments?

The person who checks to see that your evidence is of the right quality and quantity is called an assessor. This will usually be the teacher or lecturer who set the assignment or task. In order to make sure that all the assessors in your school or college are assessing at the same level, one or more of the team of teaching staff will take on the role of the internal verifier. If you feel that your work has not been fairly assessed, you can appeal to the internal verifier to look at your work again. Each shool or college will have its own appeals procedure which you should follow.

Acknowledgements

The author and publishers would like to thank the following for permission to reproduce copyright material: CSO for Figure 1.1; The Grand Hotel, Brighton for Figures 2.3, 2.7, 2.14, 2.15, 3.8, 3.10, 3.15, 3.19, 3.21 and 4.2; the Greenalls Group for Figure 3.2; Lloyds TSB Bank plc for Figures 3.22, 3.23 and 3.24; Innsite Hotel Services Limited for Figures 3.25, 3.26 and 3.30; and Whitehall Hotel, Broxted, Essex for Figure 3.31.

An introduction to the hospitality and catering industry

1

This unit will provide you with a good understanding of the scale and scope of the hospitality and catering industry. You will investigate organizations and outlets in different sectors of the industry and present your findings regarding:

- **the scale and scope of the industry sectors nationally**

- **the external and internal influences on organizations and outlets**

- **current and future trends of the industry**

- **how to investigate and collect different sources of information**

The scale and scope of hospitality and catering nationally

The hospitality and catering industry provides food, drink and accommodation to huge numbers of people from abroad as well as people who live and work in the UK. With a turnover of over £40,000 million, the industry contributes some 4 per cent of the total national income. By employing over 1.88 million people, it provides almost 6 per cent of total employment in the economy. The industry is relatively labour intensive, with wage costs at over 43 per cent of total costs (i.e. wage costs plus bought-in costs).

The nearest official definition of the industry is 'hotels and catering', but this excludes important activities such as sports and gaming clubs, and convalescent and rest homes. Even the official figures for the hospitality and catering industry (HCI) may not include some relevant activities, such as canteens operating within a factory or office block.

When considering which outlets to study, bear in mind that outlets where accommodation is provided normally have a greater range of facilities and services than those that simply offer catering.

Historical context

The increase in mobility of people generally has been a major factor in the growth in demand for hospitality and catering. The mansion houses, palaces and castles of the gentry originally provided these facilities for the ruling classes; indeed the members of the royal courts spent most of the year staying at each other's establishments. Monasteries offered accommodation and sustenance to other travellers on a very simple basis.

The present structure of the HCI owes much to developments in the various modes of **transport** over time. Each new form of transport brought with it an increased demand for hospitality and catering outlets:

- ✪ **stage coaches – coaching inns (many are now hotels)**
- ✪ **railways – station hotels, buffets, refreshment cars**
- ✪ **motorcars – motels, roadside cafes, etc.**
- ✪ **aeroplanes – airport facilities, in-flight catering**

Alongside developments in transport, changes in **working**, **studying** and **recreational** patterns of behaviour have encouraged further growth in the demand for hospitality and catering activities.

- ✪ **Catering in workplaces and colleges has increased as more people work or study further from home**
- ✪ **Accommodation in seaside guesthouses, hotels, holiday camps, etc. has increased as more holidays are taken**
- ✪ **Catering at sports centres, etc. has increased as more people participate in leisure activities**

There has also been a progressively greater need for **social facilities** for larger, more diverse populations, for example:

- ✪ **homes for those with special needs – the elderly, prisoners, etc.**
- ✪ **home services – meals on wheels, etc.**

The function of the hospitality and catering industry

In order to make sense of such a diverse industry, it is necessary to look at the outcomes the industry seeks to provide and the basic functions which it undertakes.

The main function of the industry is selling:

- ✪ **the use of accommodation, in the form of rooms for sleeping or other purposes such as conferences, business meetings and receptions**
- ✪ **meals, usually for consumption on the premises**

The industry is divided into the functional work areas of:

- ✪ **food preparation**
- ✪ **food and drink sales**
- ✪ **accommodation services**
- ✪ **front office**

The structure of the hospitality and catering industry

The two main sectors of the HCI are usually taken to be the **commercial** and **catering services** sectors.

✪ The **commercial sector** includes those aspects of hospitality and catering activities which are provided with the primary objective of making profit (for example hotels, contract catering, etc.).

✪ The **catering services sector** includes the provision of hospitality and catering activities which are secondary to the main function of the outlet (for example in-house catering provided to car workers). The latter may be heavily subsidized, the primary objective being to attract and retain a well-motivated workforce.

The distinction between the two sectors is becoming more blurred, as contracting out within the public and private sectors means for profit organizations are also providing the various catering services. It is the commercial sector which will be the main focus of interest in this unit.

The two main sectors can in turn be divided into sub-sectors. These consist of outlets which are similar in their function and operation (see Figure 1.1). We will consider aspects of scale for each of these sub-sectors and will start by looking at the largest, namely hotels.

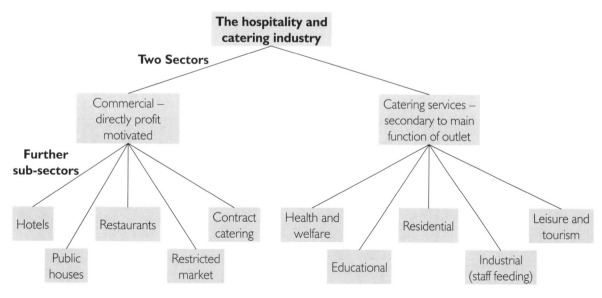

Figure 1.1   *Sectors of the industry*
Courtesy of CSO

The commercial sector

Hotels

The main function of hotels is the sale of accommodation. This sector includes a wide variety of establishments, from multinational chain hotels (five-star), through four-star and three-star hotels, business hotels, motels, to guesthouses and even holiday camps and villages.

With a turnover in excess of £13,800 million and employing around 259,000 people, the hotel sector makes an important contribution to the economy. This sector also plays an important part in improving the UK's balance of payments by providing services to tourists from overseas.

Small hotels and guesthouses cater for the greatest volume of people: 44.1 per cent of all **resident stays** take place in establishments with less than ten rooms, and 83.1 per cent in establishments with less than 24 rooms. Indeed, hotels with over 200 rooms have only 0.7 per cent of all resident stays. Nevertheless, the medium and large hotel groups or chains are an important feature of the sector. The top ten hotel groups listed in Figure 1.2 between them account for 43.1 per cent of the total market (i.e. all residents).

It is hardly surprising that the majority of resident stays occur in small to medium-size hotels, since it is these hotels which dominate the market. Indeed, 92 per cent of the 53,500 hotel outlets in the UK provide fewer than 25 rooms.

	Hotels	*Rooms*
1 Granada	327	29,816
2 Whitbread	253	16,727
3 Thistle	95	13,197
4 Hilton	41	8,651
5 Stakis	53	8,265
6 Holiday Inn	41	8,030
7 Queens Moat	48	7,096
8 Regal	95	5,170
9 Greenalls	80	5,140
10 Jarvis	63	5,131

Figure 1.2 *Top ten hotel groups in the UK, 1998*

The regional distribution of these outlets shows that 50 per cent of the hotels with over 50 rooms are in London, with most operated by the large international groups: Hilton, Inter-Continental, etc. The remaining large hotels are mainly operated by national companies: De Vere, Cunard, Queens Moat, Savoy, etc.

Public houses

The main function of public houses is to sell alcohol. Approximately 70,000 establishments are predominantly engaged in selling alcoholic drink, largely beers, much of it to a male market. Over 318,000 people are currently employed in public houses and bars, 70 per cent of employees being female.

Public houses are either owned by a group, run by a salaried manager or by tenants, or they are free houses, independently owned and run. Public houses are fast becoming big providers of cooked meals and hot snacks as customers trade down from restaurants in favour of budget meals. Sales of non-food items such as alcohol, tobacco and accommodation by pubs and restaurants total around £8.5 billion – roughly the same as eat-in food sales.

However, the overall pub market in the UK is shrinking as a result of the Government's Beer Orders which followed the Monopolies and Mergers Commission report on the brewing and pub industry. Consumption of draft beer has also been falling, to the consternation of brewers. Added to this has been the greater concentration of pub ownership, and the sale or closure of many poor-quality pubs.

As the big pub operators have witnessed falling draft beer sales, they have turned to other areas to boost turnover. To pub operators and brewers such as Whitbread, food sales are becoming almost as important as beer sales. The value of pub food sales in 1999 was £4,825 million. Pub menus are offering better value for money and a wider selection of meals, and have become more creative. Many pub chains are also targeting their menu to appeal to children in an attempt to compete in the family market with the ever-popular hamburger chains. However, growth in the pub food market is concentrated in the hands of the larger operators such as Boddington, Greenalls and Grand Metropolitan.

Restaurants

The main function of restaurants is to sell food and drink, which is usually eaten on the premises but may also be taken away. The group includes restaurants, speciality restaurants (steakhouses, Chinese, Indian, etc.), fast food outlets, cafes and take-aways.

With a turnover in excess of £20,145,000, restaurants contribute over 2 per cent to the UK's national income. They employ over 603,000 people; over two-thirds of the workforce are women, and over three-quarters of these women are working part-time.

This is a very large and expanding area which includes luxury restaurants offering meals at £30 or more, as well as fast food outlets selling snacks at £1.50. There are approximately 15,000 restaurants in the UK as well as 30,000 fast food outlets and take-aways.

The number and variety of establishments continue to increase and include the steak houses, hamburger joints and pizza houses. There has also been a resurgence of sandwich bars. Some restaurants, like the Golden Egg chain, have vanished completely, but others have emerged, for example Starbucks.

Recent trends in the restaurant sector include the following:

✪ **Grazing snacks throughout the day rather than eating meals at defined times is now an accepted occurrence, hence the continued growth in the fast food sector.**

✪ **A clear distinction between eat-in and fast food continues to be difficult. Some operators have come down in favour of one market or another. For example, Pizzaland is shedding its fast food image and is very much an eat-in restaurant, but Pizza Hut is still regarded as direct competition by Burger King, McDonald's and Kentucky Fried Chicken (KFC).**

✪ **Franchising is prevalent, particularly in pizza and chicken establishments.**

✪ **Some public houses have been turned into restaurants.**

✪ **Employment in the fast food establishments particularly is mainly part-time and semi-skilled, with a high turnover.**

✪ **Restaurants employ a wide range of people, from those with no formal training to highly skilled professionals.**

Restricted market

The main function of the restricted market is the selling of food and drink to participants only, for example to those in transit from one destination to another, members of dining clubs, night clubs, etc. It is more difficult to extract data for this sector though it is undoubtedly fast growing:

✪ **Over 65 million passengers pass through UK airport terminals annually**

✪ **Over 26 million passengers use one or other cross channel routes annually**

In all these cases, the travel requirements come first and the catering must be adapted to suit the travelling priorities. A similar perspective must be adopted when catering for those in night clubs, gaming clubs, etc.

Commercial contract catering

Commercial contract caterers are specialized firms which provide food and drink service outlets for other firms or institutions. Commercial contract catering is 'for profit' and includes many large firms such as Gardner Merchant, Sutcliffe, Compass, etc.

Commercial contract caterers in Britain served more than 1,300 million meals in 1998, an increase of 17 per cent compared with the previous year according to the British Hospitality Association's (BHA) annual contract catering survey. Turnover in the UK increased by 27 per cent to £2 billion of which 10 per cent was accounted for by management fees. Turnover of UK contract caterers overseas earned another £400 million.

Expansion continues into new markets such as healthcare, education and catering for the public, the latter, in particular, being a major growth area. Between 1994 and 1999 the number of meals served to the public by commercial contract caterers rose from 5 per cent to 13 per cent of the total to represent some 120 million meals a year. This includes outlets in leisure centres, department stores, airports, railway stations, at public events and in places of entertainment.

Although there has been a dramatic decline of catering for business and industry as a proportion of the whole market, it is still by far the largest market segment for contract caterers. However, this does not reflect the structure of the food service industry as a whole as education and healthcare are bigger segments, but contract caterers have yet to penetrate those markets as fully as they have business and industry.

In terms of the number of outlets they operate, commercial contract caterers increased their share of the total food service management market from 12.2 per cent in 1992 to 20 per cent in 1999.

At the launch of the BHA survey, Jim Cartwright, chairman of the BHA's contract catering panel, said that despite the drop in the number of business and industry outlets served, growth in other markets 'makes the future prospects of contract catering very bright indeed'.

Commercial contract catering involves catering at a known cost to the host who can leave any difficulties that might occur to a caterer, rather than take on an extra concern for an establishment whose main work is elsewhere.

The catering services sector

Most contract catering services are provided in outlets where the provision of meals is not the main activity of the outlet. The term 'catering services', or increasingly 'food service management', is applied to this sector of the hospitality and catering industry. It covers such areas as feeding people at work in business and industry, catering in schools, colleges and universities, hospitals and healthcare, welfare and local authority catering and other non-profit making outlets.

As we have already noted, the definition of this sector is now becoming blurred as it increasingly includes major areas of commercial contract catering provided for members of the public. As a proportion of the total contract catering market, this 'commercial' sector is growing fast. The traditional sectors – called 'cost', 'non-profit making', 'non-commercial' or 'social' catering – continue, but because contractors are developing their interests in commercial catering, the term 'food service management' is also used to define the total contract catering industry. Estimates are that the total number of outlets in the non-commercial or cost sector, which remains the primary target for food service management companies, is 83,050. On this basis, contractors are responsible for 14.4 per cent of the entire catering market.

UK catering contractors still have some way to go before they match the average 80 per cent share of the US business and industry market. The European average, however, remains at 30 per cent.

Health and welfare outlets

This sector includes:

- ✪ **over 2,000 NHS hospitals with over 7,000,000 patients**
- ✪ **over 150 private hospitals**
- ✪ **6,000 homes run by councils**
- ✪ **3,000 privately run homes**

Although there is an increasing use of contract catering, a large sector still exists with very professionally organized health service catering. The use of cook–chill and cook–freeze with a centralized production unit has become prevalent. The traditional service of heated bulk food trolleys delivered by nurses has been mainly replaced by 'Ganymede' systems. The first cook–chill system was trade-named 'Ganymede' and this name is now used for this type of operation. The objectives were to improve quality and choice, and to relieve nurses. The service is operated centrally using a conveyor belt. Preordered meals are made up on trays and then dispatched to the wards. Ganymede uses metal pellets under the plate to keep the food hot, Helitherm uses insulation and Stellex has electric hot plates in the trolleys and the trays have holes to match.

Educational outlets

The school meal service still provides a meal each day for nearly 50 per cent of the 9.7 million schoolchildren. To cope with the large number of schools, cook–chill meals from a centralized production unit are often used with less provision at each site.

Nearly 3 million students (full- and part-time) are attending colleges. Contract catering is being increasingly used in colleges in line with government requirements for open tendering. Universities are not providing the same meal service as in the past, with many students preferring to self-cater. But in the traditional universities and colleges, meals are still formal with a high table for the Fellows and their guests, and some special dinners.

Residential outlets

Catering is made available in a variety of situations where residential care is required. This includes homes for elderly people, children's homes, the prison service and the armed forces. The money available varies but the need to provide a balanced, varied diet is constant. Contract catering is becoming more prevalent in this area.

Staff feeding in industry

This area of the industry has seen some decline, partly due to the shrinking of the large manufacturing industries and to changes in eating habits.

Industrial catering, as it used to be called, was started by the more enlightened employers who were concerned with staff welfare and could see a correlation between healthy, well-fed employees and production. It expanded during the First and Second World Wars as a means of supplying extra rations to employees in essential industries.

Today, it is part of a whole package of fringe benefits offered to employees. The catering is ancillary to the main purpose of the business and so many companies have passed it over to contractors. What is available varies from egalitarian cafeterias where everyone eats together, to a whole structure of outlets for each of the levels of staff culminating in a directors' dining-room with some of the best food and wine available anywhere. Part of the status of each employee depends upon where they can eat.

With the decline of manufacturing industry and the expansion of service industries, a large number of sandwich and snack delivery operations have emerged, with vending machines available for drinks, which are sometimes free but are usually subsidized.

Leisure and tourism outlets

There has been rapid expansion in this area which includes any catering which is carried out within recreational facilities such as:

- ✪ **sport centres, swimming pools, race tracks**
- ✪ **golf, football, cricket, snooker clubs**
- ✪ **theatres, cinemas**
- ✪ **museums, country houses, zoos, country parks**
- ✪ **amusement parks**

Again, the catering is secondary to some other activity, but it has become recognized as an important source of income and is now given much more focus than previously when it was sometimes carried out on a voluntary basis.

Tourism is at last being recognized as essential to the economy of the UK and many other countries. The foreign currency earned from tourism helps to increase the invisible exports of the country.

Activity 1.1

The increase in air travel has resulted in the continued expansion of airports, in particular around the London area. The anticipated growth in passenger numbers departing from London Stansted Airport will result in more staff being employed at the airport as well as increased numbers of passengers using local facilities. What effects is the growth at Stansted Airport likely to have on the local economy in the area of hospitality and catering? What types of catering outlets will be required in order to cope with the demand?

Employment

The hospitality and catering industry employed 1,884,000 people in 1998. Employment is increasing in what is one of the largest of the service industries.

As we looked at the various sectors within the HCI, we touched on some aspects of employment. In general, a number of patterns and trends can be identified:

✪ The industry employs more women than men, many in part-time posts, but career prospects are better in the HCI than in most other industries.

✪ The reputation of the industry for working antisocial hours is true for many sectors, but there are areas where the work is more socially accepted, for example with the increasing use of centralized production units.

✪ Promotion for entrants can be rapid and opportunities vary across the industry. There are different career patterns. Many will have moved from hotels to education and then perhaps to restaurants.

Traditionally, employment in hotels was the ambition of most entrants aiming for a qualification, but then experience in all four functional areas (see page 4) was required to gain management positions.

Today, there are a range of qualifications and various possible routes within each sector of the industry in each of the functional areas. Pay rates vary, with adjustments often made for living in and for expected levels of gratuities (tips). Some sectors, for example hospitals, have agreed national pay rates, but the norm in the industry is for no such agreements and for pay to be dependent on market forces. Most skilled and managerial posts are salaried, whereas semi-skilled and unskilled posts are waged (paid per hour/weekly). Belonging to professional associations is desirable for career development, for example:

✪ **Hotel Catering and Institutional Management Association (HCIMA) – for those interested in management**

✪ **Cookery and Food Association (CFA) – for those interested in catering management and food preparation and service, and for chefs and waiters**

✪ **Guild of Sommeliers – for wine waiters and butlers**

A pay and benefits survey carried out in the mid 1990s was probably the largest ever for the HCI. Among its results:

✪ **80 per cent of respondents were in non-salaried jobs – this was more than before and indicated increased use of casual and flexible staffing arrangements**

- **Only 14 per cent of establishments had staff with NVQs**
- **53 per cent of respondents were in pension schemes**
- **Average holiday entitlement was between 20 and 25 days**
- **Meals on duty were offered to 80 per cent of respondents**
- **Management live-out salaries averaged £16,500 – a considerable increase in real terms over the previous five years**

Staffing in the functional areas

Within the hospitality and catering industry four **functional areas** have been designated:

- **food preparation**
- **food and drink sales**
- **accommodation services**
- **front office**

Below is a brief overview of the staffing requirements in these functional areas.

Food preparation

Role: Purchasing, preparing, cooking and serving meals for sale

Staffing

Head chef	Manager – planning, leading, controlling (NVQ4)
Sous chef	Supervisory skilled professional (NVQ3)
Chef	Technician – skilled professional (NVQ2)
Assistant/commis	Trainee – semi-skilled (NVQ1)
Porter	Unskilled cleaner

Food and drink sales

Role: Selling meals and drinks to customers

Staffing

Restaurant manager	Manager – planning, leading, controlling (NVQ4)
Head waiter/ress	Supervisory skilled professional (NVQ3)
Waiter/ress	Technician – skilled professional (NVQ2)

| Assistant/commis | Trainee – semi-skilled (NVQ1) |
| Washer up | Unskilled cleaner |

Accommodation services

Role: Care of the rooms

Staffing

Head housekeeper	Manager – planning, leading, controlling (NVQ4)
Supervisor/floor housekeeper	Technician – skilled professional (NVQ3)
Room maid	Semi-skilled (NVQ1)
Cleaner	Unskilled cleaner

Front office

Role: Selling accommodation and providing administrative support

Staffing

Front office manager	Manager – planning, leading, controlling (NVQ4)
Head receptionist	Supervisory skilled professional (NVQ3)
Receptionist	Technician – skilled professional (NVQ2)
Assistant	Trainee – semi-skilled (NVQ1)
Porter	Semi-skilled (NVQ1)

Activity
1.2

Find out about the staffing in a hospitality or catering establishment and use the form in Figure 1.3 as the basis for a detailed report.

Name of outlet				
Location				
Type of outlet				
Departments e.g.	**Job titles**	**Qualification**	**Pay**	**Comment career?**
Food preparation	(i.e. head chef)	NVQ2+3	Salary	22 yrs male — Move
	3 chefs	NVQ2	Wage	18–40 2M, 1F, — Move
	1 trainee	NVQ1–2	Wage	16 M — Promotion?
	1 porter	–	Hourly rate	40 M — None
Food service				
Reception				
Accommodation				
Other – office, maintenance				
Management				
Management style Staff morale	Democratic Positive	Consultative Satisfactory	Autocratic Poor	Effective ?
Date:		Name:		

Figure 1.3 *Framework for a detailed report on staffing*

External influences on the hospitality and catering industry

The various **external** influences can be divided into four broad categories:

1 **Legislation** – the range of legal aspects which influence the conduct of a hospitality and catering outlet is expanding through Parliament, the courts and Europe

2 **The economy** – the local, national and world economic situations affect the industry, and have a greater or lesser impact on the different sectors

3 **Social changes** – changes in population structure (demographic changes) and living habits affect different sectors of the industry

4 **Technology** – greater availability of mechanization, computers and product development will affect the industry

Legislation

There have been laws and regulations controlling hospitality and catering in the past, but since the 1980s these have increased due to greater concerns about consumer protection and, in the case of catering, to particular concern about food handling. There have also been many changes in employment law. Hospitality and catering is a service industry and employs large numbers of full- and part-time workers. These employment regulations have had a considerable impact.

Membership of the European Union (EU) means that the UK is subject to laws and directives from Brussels. These have had to be assimilated and they have changed some aspects of the industry, for example wine now has to be sold in 75 cl bottles and specific details must be included on the labels – the days of an establishment providing its own-label wine with no further identification are gone.

The less direct effects of changes in VAT and in excise duty have influenced customers' behaviour and have changed the face of the industry. For example, duty on beer is now similar to that on wine. EU regulations gave the UK a choice of either reducing the duty on wine or increasing it on beer and cider. The decision was made in favour of the latter, with the increase being gradually phased in. The effect on public houses has been considerable: higher prices have resulted in loss of custom. On the other hand, there has been a growth of wine bars and of sales of wine in restaurants.

At much the same time the Monopolies Commission attacked the big brewers for not allowing enough competition in their tied and managed public houses. This also meant changes in the ownership and operation of public houses.

The economy

The local, national and worldwide economic situation is an important influence on the industry. For example, the Stock Market crash of 1987 had immediate effects on the restaurant trade in the city of London, then on many other establishments which were patronized by the high earners in the South East of England. The more widespread national economic recession of the late 1980s and the early 1990s led to many restaurant and pub closures throughout the country. The still broader worldwide recession of the early 1990s reduced the flow of tourists to the UK, again depressing the hospitality and catering industry.

Those parts of the HCI which are particularly sensitive to changes in people's income will be most directly affected by economic recession or recovery. Spending on eating out is a good example of this as people use part of any increased earnings to enjoy the luxury of eating outside their own homes. Spending on eating out grew rapidly during the mid to late 1980s when real incomes were rising fast. The growth during the mid to late 1990s was at a much slower rate as people's real incomes rose less rapidly. A reflection of this trend has been the growth in pub catering spending which is now over £4 billion and which grew by 10 per cent between 1986 and 1992.

As well as affecting tourism, the state of the world economy can influence the HCI in other ways. For example, changes in the world commodity prices of foodstuffs and drinks of various types will directly affect the costs of providing many HCI services. Trends in multinational corporate activity worldwide will also affect the national and local HCI – for example the expansion plans of McDonald's, Hilton, Forte, Grand Metropolitan, etc. and the use to which they put their huge advertising budgets.

Social changes

The industry is having to adapt in order to cope with changes in the way society is organized. The expansion of **fast food outlets**, the introduction of **food courts**, **drive thru** and **home delivery services** are all examples of innovations (or at least changes in presentation) which meet people's needs at the beginning of the 21st century. Many of these reflect the social changes towards a more mobile population, including family or social units in which two people work and where time is at a premium. In such societies there is a greater willingness to pay for 'convenience' in its many forms.

Changes in the population include more disposable income for the young and greater numbers in the older age ranges. Over 5 million women now work part-time, making convenience foods more attractive as a time-saving option. More and more people are living alone. More than a quarter of all households are one-person households – double the proportion in 1961.

Fashion in food and drink is becoming much more important. There is greater interest in ethnic foods of all types. In part this is related to an increased awareness of the benefits of healthier eating, which encourages selection from a wider range of menus. It also reflects a growing proportion of ethnic minority groups among the young. For example, over four in ten of those from the Pakistani and Bangladeshi communities are under 16 – twice the proportion of the general population.

Greater acceptance of the principle of 'disposables' within the population has encouraged the growth of automated vending operations, fast food operations, etc. The rapid growth in ownership of refrigerators and freezers in households has helped to stimulate the growth in pre-prepared foods.

Technology

Freezers, blast chillers, microwave ovens, electronic tills and the use of computers for control and accounting purposes are all seen as essential for efficient operation in many sectors. Improvements in the technologies of distribution to wholesale and retail premises have given a boost to various fresh-food sectors and to pre-prepared items. New technologies involving mechanization, automation and computerization have permitted volume production of standardized items at low cost. This has also encouraged the growth of convenience, pre-prepared foods.

Local trends

Local trends can also have an important impact on an HCI outlet. For example, demand may be **seasonal** in some localities, perhaps peaking in the tourist season. This is particularly the case in seaside resorts or other tourist centres. In peak periods the outlet may need to take on extra (part-time) staff, and also buy in extra ingredients, raw materials, etc. Operations may then be considerably scaled down in the off-peak periods.

Local demographic considerations may also exert an important influence. For example, university towns with extensive bedsit accommodation in certain neighbourhoods will often support a high proportion of take-away and fast food outlets. Students have limited time in which to cook or prepare meals but they also have limited finances, so bought-in meals must be relatively inexpensive.

Internal influences on the hospitality and catering industry

As well as the various external influences, the operational characteristics and prospects of success within the HCI will also depend on a number of **internal** factors.

Staff

There is a shortage of trained staff in the industry and this is where increased education and training is so important. The hope is that the new NVQ and Vocational A-level courses will lead to an increase in skills among staff in hospitality and catering. The industry uses a large number of part-time and casual staff who do not always have any training and may not identify with the objectives of a professional industry. Low wage culture and the reliance on tips to make up income undermine professionalism and are slow to change. The tradition of a seasonal industry has meant that there has always been a high staff turnover, which has some advantages for the individual but militates against efficiency and uniformity of product.

Management

As with all UK industry, management within the HCI is only recently becoming truly professional. The industry, with its domestic and craft background, has been slower than most to adapt to modern marketing and business methods. The influence of the American fast food chains and hotel groups, together with the increasingly difficult trading conditions of recent years, has encouraged the introduction of professional management methods.

Working conditions

The tradition within many areas of the industry was for staff to be working on split shifts, morning and evening, to be living in and to be reliant on the tips that customers left. Changes have meant that many more people are now working on straight shifts. Attempts are also being made to ensure better working conditions.

The latest EU Directives regarding part-time employees and their equal treatment with full-timers will almost certainly have an impact. Unionization in the industry has always been small. Wages Councils used to ensure a reasonable minimum wage for many employees, but these were disbanded in the 1980s giving greater influence to the 'marketplace' in determining wages. The outcome has been still lower wages for many unskilled activities but higher rewards for those with more skills.

More employers are beginning to understand the advantages of having a happier, more motivated workforce and are introducing an increasing number of staff benefits including:

✪ **meals, at least while on duty**

✪ **uniforms being provided or at least laundered or cleaned**

✪ **accommodation, which used to be normal for many hotels but now is less common**

✪ **use of establishment's facilities for leisure, staff clubs, teams, etc. (sporting and social)**

Investigating and using information sources

You will need to investigate, collect and sort information on the hospitality and catering industry and present it within agreed timescales. Sources include:

- ✪ **government and commercial publishers**
- ✪ **professional, industry and trade associations**
- ✪ **newspapers and the trade press**
- ✪ **television, video and the internet**

Information about outlets, influences on outlets, trends in the industry, jobs and employment patterns should come from a variety of sources and include statistical data. A possible source is firsthand experience of what it is like to be a customer. This will help you to learn more about the facilities and services needed and who provides them. You may learn more if, after 'being the customer', you are able to talk to the staff who provided the services. This work may be carried out as part of a group, with all members of the group visiting one outlet, or by individuals visiting outlets independently.

Resources

Creating and updating suitable information resources requires support from librarians, technicians and senior managers as well as from colleagues in the industry and elsewhere. You could collect information by carrying out investigations in small groups. In this way a valuable resource bank can be built without losing the goodwill of local industry.

Useful resources include:

- ✪ **local maps, directories, newspapers, guides and leaflets**
- ✪ **local statistical information, videos and websites focusing on outlets and jobs**
- ✪ **national maps, organizational directories and websites focusing on employment statistics**
- ✪ **publications covering the types of outlets, staffing structures, communication systems, workplace rules and the implications of legislation governing them**
- ✪ **information on EU workplace rules and the implications of legislation**

Sources of information and data

Gathering information on the operational, employment and legal aspects of any sector within the HCI will be a crucial part of many assignments relevant to your portfolio of evidence. Below are some possible sources you might consider.

Government sources

✪ *Guide to Official Statistics*, **HMSO Books, PO Box 276, London SW8 SDT**

This is perhaps the most useful starting point in any search for statistical sources. First published in 1976, and now in its fifth edition, the guide covers virtually all official government statistics and some important non-official ones.

✪ *Business Monitor* **(BM), Business Statistics Office, Cardiff Road, Newport, Gwent, NPT IXG**

Business Monitor **presents summary information on the annual census of production, with a two- to three-year time-lag. Detailed data are presented on output, employment and costs, for both establishments and enterprises in each industry group.**

✪ *Employment Gazette* **(EG), Department of Employment, Caxton House, Tothill Street, London SWIH 9NF**

Employment Gazette **is the monthly publication of the Department of Employment. Each edition contains labour market data on employment, unemployment, vacancies, industrial disputes, earnings and retail prices.**

✪ *Social Trends* **(ST), HMSO, PO Box 276, London SWS 5DT**

Social Trends **gives a detailed breakdown of patterns of household wealth, income and expenditure, together with demographic, housing and other social trends.**

Trade journals

✪ *Caterer and Hotel Keeper*
✪ *Hospitality*

Trade associations

Whether you cook, serve, buy, sell, control, clean or manage, if you work in hospitality you are one of a special group. There is a host of associations for all specialists, and here we list some of the main national ones. You may approach those of interest to you for information and data on the various activities of the members of that association.

- **British Hospitality Association**, Queens House, 55–56 Lincoln's Inn Fields, London WC2A 3BH

  Tel: 020 7404 7744, Fax: 020 7404 7799, Email: bha@bitoa.co.uk

  The BHA aims to be the voice of the hotel and catering industry.

- **Catering Industry Liaison Council**, Papermakers House, Rivenhall Road, Westlea, Swindon SN5 7BD

  Tel: 01793 886086, Fax: 01793 886182

  CILC is a liaison group of industry associations which meets regularly at the House of Commons. It currently has 12 associations in membership, representing a cross-section of the catering industry, from manufacturers and importers to local authority caterers and consultants.

- **Cookery & Food Association**, 1 Victoria Parade, 331 Sandycombe Road, Richmond-Upon-Thames, Surrey TW9 3NB

  Tel: 020 8948 3870, Fax: 020 8332 6326

  The CFA was founded by chefs in 1888, and now also has sections for waiting staff and for corporate members. Divisions around the UK and overseas hold meetings and demonstrations.

- **Hospital Caterers Association**, c/o Mrs S. Roberts, North Staffs. Hospital, Stoke on Trent, ST4 6QR

  Tel: 01782 552 790, Fax: 01782 552 731

  The aims of the association are the promotion and improvement of standards of catering in hospitals and health care in the UK and elsewhere; the education and training of people engaged in health care services; and promoting their professional interests and status.

- **Hotel & Catering International Management Association (HCIMA)**, 191 Trinity Road, London SW17 7HN

  Tel: 020 8672 4251, Fax: 020 8840 6217, Website: http://hcima.org.uk

  The HCIMA is the only internationally recognized professional association for managers and potential managers in all sectors of hospitality, from hotels, contract catering, restaurants and pubs to hospitals, schools and armed forces catering.

- **Restaurant Association**, Africa House, 64–78 Kingsway, London WC2B 6AH

  Tel: 020 7250 3222, Fax: 020 7831 8703, Website: http://ragb.co.uk

  The R A has been protecting the interests and advancing the views and opinions of independent restaurateurs for more than 28 years.

Activity 1.3

Research a local outlet and use the form in Figure 1.4, page 26, to record details of your findings.

Activity 1.4

Using Figure 1.5, page 27, produce an evaluation of a local outlet. You should consider the effectiveness of the outlet as a hospitality and catering operation rather than as a business.

Revision questions

1   List the desirable qualities and skills required in a receptionist.   (5 marks)

2   List the desirable qualities and skills required in a chef.   (5 marks)

3   List the desirable qualities and skills required in a bar supervisor.   (5 marks)

4   Give an example of a career route for a receptionist becoming a front office manager.   (8 marks)

5   Name the Act which covers health and safety in the workplace.   (2 marks)

6   Explain how celebration days, annual festivities and the seasons cause fluctuations in business.   (5 marks)

7   Explain why fluctuations in the value of UK currency against other currencies affects choice when people purchase food, drink and/or accommodation.   (5 marks)

8   Explain the difference between commercial and catering services outlets.   (5 marks)

9   What is meant by the term 'hospitality'?   (3 marks)

10 What is meant by the term 'catering'?   (3 marks)

	Survey of HCI outlet	
Name of outlet		
Location		
Type of outlet		
Ownership/Management	*Public/private company/partnership/independent*	
Turnover/Profitability		
Internal factors	Environment	*Formal/informal, friendly*
	Plan	*Open/divided*
	Décor	*Bright/relaxed/escapist*
	Menu	*Fixed/daily/A la carte/Table d'hôte*
	Drinks	*Licensed/unlicensed*
	Rooms	*Number/types: twin/double/single/suites*
Operational methods	Food service	*Table/counter/personal*
	Food production	*Cook–serve/cook–store–serve/store–serve*
	Reception	
	Accommodation	
Internal influences	Staffing	*Number* *Structure*
	Management	*Democratic/consultative/autocratic*
	Facilities	*Leisure*
External influences	Seasonal variations	
	Competition	
	Local environment	
Sources of information	Customers	*Observation/questionnaires/conversation*
	Staff	*Observation/questionnaires/interviews*
	Other	*Reports/guides*
Date:	Signature:	

Figure 1.4 *Framework for a survey*

Evaluation of

By

Strengths	Criteria	Weaknesses
	Meeting requirements Standards Customers Special needs	
	Complying with the law Hygiene Safety Licensing	
	Organization Staff Communications	
	Staff performance Social skills Technical skills Knowledge	
	Efficiency Timing Flow Accuracy	
	Value for money	
	Dealing with the unforeseen	
Reliable/Valid	*Data Collection Methods*	*Unreliable*
	Customer information Interviews	
	Questionnaires	
	Observation	

Recommendations for improvements

Policy		
Facility		
Staff		
Are recommendations	Relevant Yes/No	Cost-effective Yes/No
Comments		

Figure 1.5   *Framework for evaluating the effectiveness of an outlet*

keys to attainment

These are key skills or aspects of key skills that are central to the Introduction to the Hospitality and Catering Industry unit. The key to attainment shows that the relevant aspect of the key skill has also been achieved. You will of course need to develop and practise the key skill during your lessons and in your private studies.

Communication, level 3

When you are:	You should have achieved the following key skills evidence:
Researching information about the scale and scope of the industry, the employment patterns and occupational skills and qualities required of employees	C3.2 Read and synthesize information from two extended documents about a complex subject. One of these documents should include at least one image.
Presenting your results logically, coherently and at a level appropriate to the audience	C3.3 Write two different types of documents about complex subjects. One piece of writing should be an extended document and include at least one image.

Application of number, level 3

When you are:	You should have achieved the following key skills evidence:
Finding out about the importance of the industry nationally, including statistical information on scale and scope Finding out about employment patterns, occupational skills and qualities needed by those employed in the industry	N3.1 Plan and interpret information gained from two different types of sources, including a large data set.
Analyzing statistical information to investigate the scale and scope of the industry nationally Analyzing statistical information to explain why the industry is a major employer	N3.2 Carry out multi-stage calculations to do with: C handling statistics. Work with a large data set on at least one occasion.
Analyzing and presenting statistical information regarding the scale and scope of the industry nationally and subsequent employment patterns	N3.3 Interpret results of calculations, present findings and justify methods of interpretation. Use at least one graph, one chart and one diagram.

Signposts

These are naturally occurring opportunities for the development of key skills through your learning and assessment. You will not necessarily achieve the signposted key skill through your evidence for the Introduction the Hospitality and Catering Industry unit. You will need to develop additional evidence elsewhere to ensure that you meet the requirements of the key skills units fully.

Communication, level 3

When you are:	There may be opportunities for you to develop the following key skills evidence:
Discussing in a group the internal and external influences on business operations	C3.1a Contribute to a group discussion about a complex subject.

Information Technology, level 3

When you are:	There may be opportunities for you to develop the following key skills evidence:
Researching the scale and scope of the industry and employment patterns, occupational skills and qualities needed by employees	IT 3.1 Plan and use different sources to search for and select information required for two different purposes.
Analyzing the influences on both your chosen outlets to predict future trends	IT 3.2 Explore, develop and exchange information and derive new information to meet two different purposes.
Presenting your results	IT 3.3 Present information from different sources for two different purposes and audiences. Include at least one example of text, one example of images and one example of numbers.

Food and drink operations

This aim of this unit is to develop an understanding of food and drink operations in hospitality and catering outlets and to learn about the staff who work in these areas.

In this unit you will learn:

- **about different types of food and drink operations**
- **about the preparation, cooking and service of food and drink**
- **about different types of staff who work in food and drink operations**
- **how menu items are served to customers**

Evaluating food and drink operations

Food and drink operations are outlets which sell meals and drinks ready for consumption usually on the premises but they also include take-away outlets. The main divisions are between restaurants, bars, fast food and take-aways, and welfare and staff dining facilities. Each is different but all have inherent similarities and you need to understand these and be able to evaluate their performance. Figure 2.1 is a framework for such an evaluation.

Headings	Suggested details – highlight or cross through/fill in details
Name of outlet	....
Location	....
Type of outlet	Hotel/restaurant/fast food/canteen/other...................
Sector of industry	Commercial/catering services
Customers	Age........./description........................
Customers' requirements	Timing: urgent/non-urgent, fast/slow
	Value for money
	Coping with special needs: dietary/mobility
	Friendly service?
Layout Plan	Open/divided/logical flow
Decor	Bright/sombre
Environment	Friendly/relaxed/formal/informal
Tables	Access/fixed/flexible/material.............., shapes
	Laid up, cloths/mats, table d'hôte/à la carte
What is on offer	Breakfast/snacks/lunch/tea/dinner/supper
	Tea/coffee/soft drinks/bar/wines
	Include sample menus and drink lists
Methods of selling	Printed/display/personal/pictures/other........................

Figure 2.1 *Framework for evaluating a catering outlet*

Headings	Suggested details – highlight or cross through/fill in details
Types of food service	Table: plate/silver/gueridon/family/other.....................
	Counter: fast food/cafeteria/vending/other..................
	Personal: tray/trolley/vending/home delivery
Events	Room service/functions, buffet, banquets, outside catering
Operational control	Till/check/bill/triplicate + bills/computer/other...........
Food production	Cook–Serve/Cook–store–serve................................. Access: direct/over hotplate/by lift/other....................
Staffing	Numbers........../structure.. Uniform: smart/appropriate/complete Hygiene: personal/practices Practical skills: preparation/carrying/serving/clearing Personal skills: communication/responsive/knowledge Working conditions
Hygiene	Premises
Safety	Any obvious hazards........................Feel safe? yes/no
Security	Customers' belongings
Legality	Display of menu/licensing/other................................
Monitoring of customer	Personal/questionnaires/none
Effects of external factors	Competition Seasonality
The future?	Trends, changes planned
Is it successful?	Satisfying customers' needs

Figure 2.1   *(cont'd)*

Drink →	Delivery point	Cellar/store		→		Customer area
Food →	→	Store →	Preparation →	Cooking →	Service →	

Figure 2.2   *The workflow in food and drink operations*

When evaluating food and drink operations, you would begin by looking at the overall plan of the establishment. This needs to be logical with clearly identified sections and a good workflow (see Figure 2.2).

Traditionally there has been a division between the backstage work – preparing and cooking – and the front of house – selling and customer service. However, this is not true of all outlets and it varies depending on service methods and operation.

The co-ordination and co-operation between all members of staff, who are all looking to satisfy customers through the provision of dishes and drinks, has been described as the **total meal experience**.

Activity 2.1

Undertake a simple survey of food and drink operations in your local area. Look for different types of operations, from hotel restaurants, bars and banqueting through traditional restaurants, speciality restaurants (pizza, Chinese, Indian, fish) to hot potato stalls, and, if relevant, meals served in the hospital and on work premises.

Food preparation and cooking

Food preparation is the cleaning, cutting, measuring and mixing which may be required to change ingredients into dishes.

Cooking is the processing of food by heat to make it more palatable and easier to eat, as well as making it safer and longer lasting.

Many outlets produce food items from fresh, dried, chilled and frozen commodities, using traditional methods. Increasingly, some food and drink outlets, for example 'branded' type restaurants, are preparing and cooking food items in centralized kitchens and storing the food until it is needed.

Food preparation and cooking systems are arrived at after considering the customers, their needs and wants, and the most cost-effective means of realizing these. There are different methods which can be used separately or together to achieve these objectives. The main methods can be divided between cook–serve and cook–store–serve. Each of these can again be subdivided and fitted to particular situations. The food which will be served can range from a simple snack to a six-course meal.

Food preparation and cooking methods

Cook–serve

This provides food which is ready for sale. The main cook–serve methods are as follows:

1 **Cook to order – dishes cooked when ordered**
   Operational features   food cooked in kitchen when ordered
   Advantages   simple, presentation possible
   Disadvantages   pressure at service times, wastage
   Examples of outlets   speciality and gourmet restaurants

2 **Call order – prepared food cooked in view of customers**
   Operational features   food cooked on back bar unit, griddle, fryer, grill, etc.
   Advantages   simple, quick
   Disadvantages   dishes take up space on tables
   Examples of outlets   cafes, steak bars, pizza parlours

3 **Batch – food prepared and cooked in bulk**
   Operational features   food of limited range ready for fast service; hotplates, bains-marie, etc. used for storage

Figure 2.3 *Breakfast buffet*
Courtesy of The Grand Hotel, Brighton

Advantages	speed of service for larger numbers, presentation possible, customer can choose from food display
Disadvantages	spoilage, wastage
Examples of outlets	traditional restaurants, cafeterias and banqueting

Cook–store–serve

Storage is an important aspect here. The main cook–store–serve methods are as follows:

1 **Cook–chill – prepared and cooked dishes stored by refrigeration**

Operational features	food prepared, cooked and stored at chilled temperature of 0–3°C until required (three days maximum storage); blast chiller needed as well as refrigerated storage
Advantages	staff employed at even work rate for normal working hours; standardization and economies of scale possible
Disadvantages	uniformity, risk of food poisoning
Examples of outlets	staff feeding, school meals, hospitals

Cook–chill systems involve elements of a factory-style operation with production line techniques and high levels of mechanization. Cook–chill equipment varies widely, particularly in relation to the size of the operation, and technological developments continue to improve ease of use and economy.

The methods of regeneration and packaging show considerable diversity. Regeneration equipment can be based on microwave, infrared, high-pressure steam or forced convection technology. Food can pass through the cook–chill cycle in a number of packaging materials, including thermoplastic, porcelain, china, ceramic, stainless steel, aluminium foil and disposable board. Recent developments have produced containers in which the food can be cooked, sealed, chilled, regenerated and served. The containers are then discarded. This not only speeds up the operation, but the minimal handling of open food reduces the risk of contamination.

2   Cook–freeze – prepared and cooked dishes stored frozen

Operational features	as cook–chill, except stored after blast freezing to −18°C; blast freezer and freezer storage required
Advantages	as cook–chill but longer storage (up to six months)
Disadvantages	more expensive equipment needed; quality can suffer
Examples of outlets	as cook–chill though less common

Cook–freeze is a catering system based on conventional cooking followed by rapid freezing to below −18°C. Food is held at this temperature during storage and transport with subsequent regeneration (reheating) immediately prior to service. A blast freezer is needed for rapid cooling of food and additional freezers are required for storing frozen foods. Packaging is also required, which is strong enough to avoid damage and will stop food drying out in the freezer.

The massive amount of storage space needed for a catering unit to freeze and keep cooked food makes this a less attractive prospect to the caterer than cook–chill and *sous vide*. If frozen food is required it is more likely that caterers will negotiate specifications with food manufacturers and buy in as needed. Indeed, this is what is happening in the larger hospitals and in some expanding contract catering firms.

3   *Sous vide* – dishes stored in vacuum packing

Operational features	food stored in vacuum packaging before or after cooking and chilled to a temperature of 0–3°C until required (21 days maximum storage); special double layered plastic used for the pouches that are non-toxic, heat stable, and exclude oxygen to reduce spoilage; pouches are heat sealed

Advantages	staff employed at even work rate for normal working hours, standardization and economies of scale possible, longer shelf life allows more flexibility (up to 21 days)
Disadvantages	high cost of equipment, uniformity, risk of food poisoning
Examples of outlets	hospitals (for diets in particular), à la carte menu selections

Planning for successful food preparation and cooking

The following aspects must be considered when planning a successful procedure for preparing and cooking food:

1	**Setting of objectives**	Customer satisfaction – Who are they? Provision of quality Enhancement of reputation
2	**Planning**	Financial targets and use of financial resources Rostering staff Ordering materials Contingency plans in case of problems
3	**Forecasting**	Numbers expected
4	**Co-ordinating**	Co-operation with others, i.e. food service, housekeeping
5	**Organizing**	To satisfy objectives To utilize equipment To process materials To use staff efficiently
6	**Leading**	Set example Gain respect Delegate Give praise
7	**Controlling**	Set standards Communicate to staff Measure performance Compare with standards Take corrective action if necessary
8	**Evaluating performance**	Give feedback Ensure any improvements are recorded for future action

Benefits of and constraints upon food preparation and cooking

Benefits

The benefits will include the pleasure and success derived from pleasing customers with the standards of food produced. The communication of that positive feedback is important in any organization. In small facilities it can be achieved firsthand, but in larger establishments there needs to be an effective means of communicating compliments as well as complaints from customers to members of staff.

Constraints

The dishes prepared and cooked need to be appropriate to customers of the facility and not just to the whim of the chef.

The sales price, which is directly related to the cost and usually dependent on a fixed percentage (mark-up on cost), will need to be set at levels acceptable to the market (the customers). The ability to produce appropriate items will be dependent on the cost base permitted as well as on the availability of staff with necessary skills and of the equipment needed to achieve the required outcomes. The design and layout of the food production and cooking area and its relationship to the service point will be critical.

Hygiene

Food production has to be concerned at all times with the essential requirements of the law and best practice regarding health, hygiene and safety of customers, staff, the premises (including fire precautions) and the food which is being produced. This requires adherence to the recommended safeguards and good practice, particularly regarding food handling. Constant monitoring and regular safety checks are needed to ensure maintenance of these standards. Hygiene is considered in more detail in Unit 5 Safety, Security and the Environment.

Food storage

Where storage is an important element in the process, appropriate methods must be adopted (see Figure 2.4).

Storage must be kept clean and stock rotation used to ensure that items are used on a first in first out basis and before 'Use by' and 'Best by' dates.

Item	Storage	Time	Comments
Dried	Dry	Up to 12 months	
Freeze dried	Dry	Up to 12 months	
Chilled	Refrigerate 3–5°C	3 days maximum	
Fresh meat etc.	Refrigerate 3–5°C	Up to 3 days	
Fresh vegetables, fruit	Cold room 6–8°C	1–3 days	
Sous vide	Refrigerate 3–5°C	Up to 20 days	Heat sealed in pouches
Canned	Dry	3–12 months	Check date on can
Smoked	Refrigerate 3–5°C	Up to 10 days	
Frozen	Freeze below –18°C	3–6 months	

All items when purchased must be checked for quantity, quality and temperature. If they do not conform to standard do not accept – return and demand replacement. Look for obvious damage, unpleasant smell and cleanliness of delivery vehicle.

Food types	Pointers for quality
Frozen	Below –13°C
Meat	Fat should be firm; flesh firm; less fat in young and free range, grass fed
Fish	Bright eyes, gills; flesh firm
Vegetables	Crisp, firm; not too dirty

Figure 2.4 *Storage of food ingredients*

Stocks should be kept as low as possible to ensure money is not tied up unnecessarily and wastage is kept to a minimum.

Preparation processes

The following are the main preparation processes:

- ✪ **measuring** – important to achieve result and for portion control
- ✪ **mixing** – combining dry ingredients
- ✪ **blending** – use of electric blender to liquidize or chop
- ✪ **whisking** – to incorporate air
- ✪ **cutting** – dividing ingredients evenly
- ✪ **chopping** – reducing to small pieces

Cooking processes

Some common techniques used during cooking are:

❂ **blanching** – placing food in cold or boiling water and bringing to the boil; used to remove unwanted flavours and impurities, to soften and to preserve colour

❂ **refreshing** – plunging into cold/iced water to stop further cooking

❂ **marinading** – immersing in a flavoured liquid to tenderize and add flavour

❂ **basting** – assisting in even cooking and colour by coating food during cooking with sauce or oil

❂ **barding** – adding fat to surface of meat to improve flavour and palatability

❂ **larding** – inserting strips of fat into meat using a needle to improve flavour and palatability

The correct process needs to be chosen to cook food in order to ensure safety, palatability and the required texture and appearance of the completed dish. Each process has its own features with steps to follow to ensure best results.

The processes are often sub-divided into dry and wet methods:

Dry processes

1 **Roasting**: This involves cooking with oil or fat in an oven or on a spit. Roasting results in high weight loss but attractive cooked flavours. Basting, barding or larding may be used. Tender joints of meat, poultry and vegetables such as potatoes and parsnips may be roasted in a tray or on a trivet (small rack). Cooking is mainly due to convection. Joints or poultry may be roasted on a spit with direct radiated heat.

2 **Grilling**: This involves cooking individually portioned tender foods by direct radiated heat. Foods such as steaks, chops and supremes (the fillet of chicken, etc.) are cooked quickly, without the necessary addition of fat. Some foods may be marinaded prior to cooking to add an attractive cooked flavour.

Steaks can be cooked to order as follows:

❂ **blue – very lightly cooked, 60°C, blue, red flesh**

❂ **rare –** *saignant*, **65°C, pink, red flesh**

❂ **medium –** *à point*, **cooked 70°C, pink flesh**

❂ **well done –** *bien cuit*, **80°C, firm, no blood**

Broiling and barbecuing are both American forms of grilling.

3 **Baking**: Mainly used for flour products with moisture such as bread and cakes, baking is a dry cooking process in an oven. Cooking is due to convection.

4 **Frying**: This is a quick dry cooking process using oil or fat. Small items are often coated with batter, flour or breadcrumbs.

Shallow frying involves cooking on a pre-heated metal surface with a minimum of oil or fat. This process is used for tender quality items such as fillets of fish, shellfish, small tender cuts of meat and poultry, made-up cutlets and pancakes and examples include fish meunière and sauté meat or vegetables.

Food may be fried on a griddle – a flat or grooved metal plate. Stir-frying involves very quick frying of small pieces of meat, fish or vegetables, usually in a pan. A Bratt pan is used for large-scale shallow frying.

Deep frying involves cooking food that is submerged in hot fat or oil. Careful thermostatic control is necessary to suit the items being cooked. The maximum temperature is 195°C. Extra care is required due to the high temperatures and liquid hot oil. Baskets and spiders are used to contain the food during frying. All foods must be dry before cooking for safety reasons. Foods and are often coated before frying. Blanching may be carried out first, particularly before frying potatoes.

Wet processes

I **Boiling**: This involves cooking food that is immersed in boiling liquid that is often not consumed. Boiling is often used to tenderize food by breaking down or softening the starch, protein and fibrous material (for example large tough joints and poultry, vegetables, dried cereals and pulses). Boiling from cold is used to remove impurities and is safer. Immersing food into boiling liquid is quicker and often essential to preserve colour (green vegetables) and to prevent starch sticking (pastas).

2 **Poaching**: This involves cooking in a liquid below boiling point.

Deep poaching: Mainly larger tender items are immersed in liquid, which is not usually made use of in the dish, for example salmon cooked in a *court bouillon* (spiced vinegar water) or pears in a stock syrup (sweetened water).

Shallow poaching: Individually portioned tender foods are cooked in a minimum of flavoured liquid which will be used to make the finished dish, for example fillets of sole are poached in white wine which is then reduced and thickened perhaps with a liaison (whisked egg yolk) and butter, before being coated over the fish.

3 **Braising**: Food is half covered with a sauce and cooked in the oven. Traditionally used for large joints of beef, ham, etc., braising is now more often used for individually portioned items such as liver, sweetbreads and onions. This method tenderizes and adds flavour to food.

4   **Steaming**: This involves cooking in water vapour (steam). Steaming can often be used instead of boiling and it has the advantage that items do not needing draining. Food can also be pressurized to increase the speed of cooking. There are particular dishes that can only be processed this way, for example the traditional steam sponges and puddings.

5   **Stewing**: This involves cooking small pieces of tough food in a minimum of liquid for a relatively long time. Stewing preserves all the flavour, as the dish is served complete with the cooking liquid, for example ragout of beef, fricassee of chicken, ratatouille, compote of fruit.

6   **Microwave cooking**: Cooking is via the activation of loose molecules in a food. Liquid does not need to be added as it is present in nearly all foods. No cooked effect is apparent on the food. This is a very fast method of cooking small items and is also excellent for providing a boost of heat. Microwave cooking can be combined with cooking in a convection oven or under a grill to produce a 'browning' or 'cooked' effect.

Menu development

Another key factor contributing to a successful food preparation and cooking policy involves menu development. The type of menu and variety of dishes offered depends upon the type of facility and the market segment which is of primary concern to the outlet.

Planning a menu

The menu should be planned in conjunction with the customers, either individually (if for a particular function) or through market research, in order to provide the meal experience required. It is important to liaise with other staff concerned with food service and control.

Menu formats and composition

The menu can be arranged so customers purchase individual dishes, each separately priced (à la carte). This provides an opportunity for increasing average spend. Greater range and menu complexity can, however, lead to higher costs.

Another option for the menu is for customers to purchase a meal package with limited choices and a fixed price (table d'hôte). There are fewer possibilities for increasing sales but easier planning and control can reduce costs. Banquet or function menus are of this format with little or no choice for prearranged numbers. Banquet menus are agreed with the customer in advance. They allow tightest control.

The following considerations should be taken into account when composing a menu, the aim of which is to achieve customer satisfaction:

✪ **the customers – what are their needs and wants?**

✪ **costs – usually within set limits, calculated as a percentage of the selling price**

✪ **staff – their ability to prepare, cook and serve the meal**

✪ **time – for staff to prepare, cook and serve the food and for customers to eat**

✪ **equipment – availability and spread of usage**

✪ **ingredients – availability and usage of items in stock and seasonal fare**

✪ **balance – of nutritionally lighter and heavier foods, cold and hot, texture and colour**

Figure 2.5 on page 46 shows the different courses in a traditional menu.

Special diets

It has become increasingly important to cater for individuals who have special requirements in order to develop and retain customer loyalty. Figure 2.6 on page 47 summarizes some of the important dietary requirements.

Consistency

Customers who have enjoyed particular dishes will have expectations of that quality or style being maintained on repeat visits. In other words an element of consistency is important to the success of food preparation and cooking. Rather than merely depending on the whim of the chef, it is therefore important that standard recipes are provided and adhered to for particular dishes.

The advantages of standard recipes may be set out as follows:

✪ **Portion yields are predetermined and therefore there is more efficient cost control**

✪ **Standards are more consistent with better quality control**

Order	Name	Description	Dish example
	Canapés	Cocktail snacks before a meal	Prawn bouche
1	Hors d'oeuvres	Dishes to stimulate the appetite	Prawn cocktail
2	Soups	Liquid appetizers	Beef consommé
3	Egg and farinaceous	Egg and cereal based dishes	Ham omelette Spaghetti napolitaine
4	Fish	Fish dishes	Cod mornay
5	Entrées	Small cuts of meat complete with sauce and garnish	Chicken curry
6	Roasts	Traditionally only poultry or game with a side salad	Roast duckling with orange salad
	Sorbet	Refreshing 'water' ice, served between courses as a break	Champagne sorbet
7	Relevés	Large joints served with vegetables	Boiled beef
8	Vegetables	Hot vegetables or salads	Asparagus with butter sauce
9	Sweet	Prepared pudding or sweet	Cream caramel
10	Savoury	Traditional small and spicy dish	Welsh rarebit
11	Dessert	Fresh fruit	Grapes, apple, etc.
	Coffee	Not a course, served after a meal	
	Petits fours	Small sweet items served with coffee	Mints, Turkish delight, glazed fruits

Figure 2.5 *Courses in traditional menus*

✪ **Purchase specifications can be standardized**

✪ **Menu planning is assisted, particularly where nutritional data is included**

✪ **Staff induction and training is simplified**

In some ways, portion control is also an aspect of consistency. The portion policy of an establishment will be determined according to the kind of catering operation. For example, with a large chain such as McDonald's, the portion control policy is centrally directed. At the other extreme, a small hotel's portion control policy will be less formally determined. It is important to realize, however, that even the relatively small operation will have a large turnover as well as a narrow profit margin, so a firm and consistent portion size and costing policy is essential to stay in business. Differences in portion sizes, however, may operate in the same establishment between table d'hôte and à la carte menus.

Food	Vegetarian	Vegan	Jewish	Hindu	Sikh	Buddhist	Islamic	Healthy
Alcohol	yes	yes	yes	no	no	no	no	limit[1]
Tea, coffee	yes	yes	yes	yes	no	yes	yes	yes
Animal fats	no	no	kosher[2]	some	some	no	halal[2]	restrict
Poultry	no	no	kosher	some	some	no	halal	yes
Pork/bacon	no	no	no	no	no	no	no	yes
Beef	no	no	kosher	no	no	no	halal	yes
Lamb	no	no	kosher	some	yes	no	halal	yes
Shellfish	some	no	no	some	some	no	no	yes
Fish	some	no	some round	some	some	some	some round	yes
Eggs	yes	no	yes	some	yes	some	yes	yes
Milk/yoghurt	yes	no	yes[3]	yes	yes	yes	yes	low fat
Nuts/pulses	yes	yes	yes	yes	yes	yes	yes	yes
Vegetables	yes	yes	yes	yes	yes	yes	yes	yes
Fruit	yes	yes	yes	yes	yes	yes	yes	yes

[1] 21 units for men, 14 units for women per week
[2] Prepared under strict religious rules
[3] Not with meat

Figure 2.6 *Dietary requirements*

Production plan

The production plan for a meal should start with the time and date of the meal required. It should then work backwards to the date at which organization will need to commence. Time should be allowed for problems but critical dates and times that must be achieved need to be known. The planner/organizer may be ill or otherwise occupied and others will need to know this information.

The planner should:

- ✪ **Delegate the parts** – give responsibility to others for parts of the operation.
- ✪ **Communicate** so that all members of the team know what is happening and feel involved.

- ✪ **Decide on the critical factors in advance**, i.e. the acquisition of ingredients and special equipment. The use of as many items as possible from own stocks will be advisable but fresh ingredients may be required. Each establishment uses different suppliers and therefore has different lead times. These should be checked and taken into account. Some foods are better prepared and even cooked the day before. Others may not be – for safety or quality factors.
- ✪ **Ensure there is sufficient safe storage** if planning to pre-prepare.
- ✪ **Use standard recipes if at all possible**. Establishments will have standardized recipes for each dish, with costings and perhaps photographs. If not, a detailed recipe and method for each dish should be produced which has been tested. Experimentation is fun, but is not to be overdone, nor mixed in with food production. The timing of the meal needs to be taken into account when deciding on recipes.
- ✪ **Produce an order of work** for each section of the operation.
- ✪ **Produce a master**, with the critical times highlighted.
- ✪ **Communicate with staff** and with others involved and personally ensure they understand.
- ✪ **Supervise staff** to ensure that the plan is working.

Staffing: food preparation and cooking

The following skills are required to prepare and cook food:

- ✪ **organizational**
    - forecasting – demand, timing
    - planning – ordering ingredients for menus, effective use of resources
    - organizing – equipment, staff, materials to achieve objectives of quality and profit (or cost control)
    - control – of ingredients, of timing
- ✪ **preparing** – for example weighing, measuring
- ✪ **cooking** – for example grilling, boiling, poaching
- ✪ **manipulative** – for example knife skills, piping and decorating, cooking
- ✪ **motivational** – leading other staff in providing quality
- ✪ **presentational** – artistic, creative
- ✪ **personal** – for example pride in high quality of work, ensuring good hygiene

These will need to be backed up with knowledge of the establishment's procedures and of the legal responsibilities, particularly as regards health, safety and hygiene.

Staffing structure

The appropriate combination of the number and quality of staff is vital in the food preparation and cooking process. The following are some of the staff required for this process together with their role and the appropriate qualification needed:

- **Head chef**: This is the head of the staff in a large operation. The head chef undertakes management, planning, organizing and controlling. He or she might be responsible to the food and beverage manager or might report direct to the general manager. (NVQ 4, CG 706/3)

- **Sous chef**: The leader of the working team reports to the head chef and is responsible for organizing, leading, co-ordinating and controlling the work of staff. The *sous chef* works in the kitchen and undertakes some practical activities such as supervising preparation and cooking, and checking dishes leaving the kitchen for quality as well as quantity. (NVQ 3 or CG 706/2/3)

- **Section chef (*chef de partie*)**: The section chef is a skilled operative who conducts the preparation and cooking of traditional sections of the range such as pastry and larder. (NVQ 2/3, CG 706/2/3)

- **Assistant/commis**: A trainee or part-time member of staff assists section chefs. (NVQ 1/2, CG 706/1)

- **Kitchen porter/washer up/cleaners**: These staff are employed to clean and to wash up, etc. and work under a skilled member of staff. (Basic Hygiene Certificate)

Food and drink service

Food and drink service is the front of house component which involves selling and providing appropriate service to complete the meal experience for the customers. Although this component of the operation is treated separately it is important that there is co-operation and co-ordination with the food preparation component as the end result of both is the satisfaction of customers. The ideal would be a seamless organization with all parts geared to the end result, but specialization and division of labour have caused artificial barriers to be erected between sections of organizations.

Traditional food service methods involve the use of professional skills, for example those needed for silver or gueridon service. In recent years, there have been changes both in the way people eat and drink in restaurants and in the way food and drink is served. These changes include greater emphasis on staff having excellent presentation and customer service skills, as well as customers self-selecting food and drink from a food court rather than being served. This section covers how food and drink items are served in outlets and will enable you to compare different food and drink service systems.

Types of food and drink service

There are three methods of food and drink service:

Figure 2.7 *Traditional restaurant*
Courtesy of The Grand Hotel, Brighton

○ **table**

○ **counter**

○ **personal**

Figure 2.8 on page 52 briefly reviews the characteristics of each method, its operation, the skills and resources involved, cost factors and types of customer need met.

Although these are the three main methods, there are also ways of distinguishing between different **types** of service: **price level** and **service style** are used to classify different types of service.

Sales and service of drinks will be an integral part of many outlets as drinks usually provide better profit margins than food because the preparation and wastage costs are less. Figure 2.9 on page 53 provides details of the production and service of alcoholic drinks (see also Appendix on page 251).

Gueridon service

Figure 2.8 briefly details a range of different methods of service which can be used individually or selectively to achieve best presentation and customer satisfaction. One table service method which has a wide range of specific requirements and skills is gueridon service.

Here we consider gueridon service (service from a side-table or trolley) in terms of its characteristics and some common dishes offered (see Figure 2.10 on pages 53 and 54):

○ **Advantages – promotes sales, gives customers confidence, allows customer participation, allows staff to show skill, provides extra service**

○ **Disadvantages – cost, space, staff, equipment, time**

○ **Equipment – small tables or trolleys (may have built-in lamp), *flambé* lamps (gas or spirit), hot plate, suzette pans (silver and copper), sharpened knives, restaurant china and silver**

○ **Usage chef and commis involved, gueridon pushed or carried to table – stays on table until service is finished, filleting and carving carried out on a plate or board**

Service preparation

All operations will require proper preparation. Figure 2.11 on page 55 outlines a probable range of preparation activities and should be used as a checklist to ensure all activities are completed. All operations benefit from having such a form, which will need to be reformatted to suit each outlet.

Methods	Description	Skills	Resources	Cost factors	Customer needs	Comments
Table	Meals served to seated guests	Personal carrying				
Plate	Preplated in kitchen	Personal carrying		Low, exact portions	Fast, simple, plate presentation	From cafes to luxury restaurants nouvelle cuisine
Family	Dishes on table	Personal carrying	Dishes	Higher, less portion control	Sociable	Ethnic restaurants: Chinese, Indian
Silver	Served using spoon and fork	Using spoon and fork	Dishes	High, slower	Impression of extra service	Traditional/banquets
Gueridon	Served from side-table/trolley	Using spoon and fork, flambé, carving, etc.	Dishes, pan lamps, etc.	Very expensive, slow	Individual attention	Very specialist
Counter	Collected by guest			Lower		
Cafeteria	Single long display counter	Portioning	Fixed counter	High turnover, low cost	Fast, simple	Impulse buying from display
Freeflow	Multiple counters	Portioning	Fixed counter	Higher turnover	Faster	Loses full display
Buffet	Set up in room		Low		Fast, simple	Informal functions
Fast food	Take-away with eat-in area	Speed	Disposables	High turnover	Limited choice, quick	
Personal	Delivered					
Tray	Assembled meal provided	Organization	Trays, etc.	High cost	Available where needed	Hospitals (Ganymede), hotel rooms, airlines
Trolley	Brought to guest		Trolleys	Low cost	Delivered in house	Offices, hospitals
Home delivery		Organization	Transport	Variable	Delivered to house	Pizza, etc., Meals on Wheels
Vending	From a machine		Machines	Low unit cost	24hr, position as required	Hot, cold, snacks, meals, drinks

Figure 2.8 *Methods of food service*

Name	Origin	Addition	Alcohol	Measure	Glass	Service
Beer	Cereal	Yeast	3–6	$\frac{1}{2}$ pint	250 ml/10 fl oz jug	
Cider	Apples		5–8	$\frac{1}{2}$ pint	250 ml/10 fl oz	
Wine	Grapes		8–15	125 ml	Paris goblet	Chill white, rosé, sparkling; reds at 16–18 °C
Liqueur wine	Grapes	Alcohol	15–24	50 ml	75 ml glass	Aromatized wines often diluted
Spirit	Anything fermentable	Distilled	40	25 ml	Tumbler	Except Scotch whisky or brandy, usually with ice and diluted
Liqueur	Spirit	Flavour	18–60	25 ml	1 oz glass	

Figure 2.9 *Alcoholic drinks: their production and service*

Course	Options	Serving instructions
Hors d'oeuvres	Orange Melon (charantais) Melon (honeydew) Avocado Cocktails	Slice end, hold on fork, section, sugar Cut top, remove pips, sweeten Segment, remove pips Cut lengthways, stone, prawns? Assemble, sauce, garnish
Soups	Cold Gazpacho Hot Germiny Extrait de boeuf à la crème Consommé au Xeres	Finish, add cream Assemble Add cream or sherry, etc. when appropriate Consommé, liaised cream, yolks, sorrel and butter Squeeze steak (press) add consommé and cream Flame sherry in ladle, float in cups
Eggs	Scrambled	
Pasta		Finish in butter, cheese, sauce and garnish
Fish Filleted fish	Grenouilles (frog's legs) Homard (lobster) Scampi Sole Colbert Trongon or Darne Trout	Sauté, finish meunière Pre-cook, re-heat, *flambé*? finish with cream Lobster sauce, tomato etc. Grilled: use two forks, easing side fillets from back Sauced: loosen, remove bone Remove head, ease out central backbone Twist off skin with fork, skewer bone Cut skin lengthways, lift off; can be filleted
Cold meats	Steak Tartare	Chopped steak, onion, capers, egg, vinegar, oil, seasoning, bound, garnish, raw egg yolk, anchovy

Figure 2.10 *Traditional gueridon dishes*

Course	Options	Serving instructions
Carving meats	Chicken	Remove legs, cut half of breast and wing, portion other half
	Poussin	Whole or halved
	Duck	Traditional: horizontal slices breast only (two portions); Modern: as per chicken, leg joint, use
	Game	Usually only breast; or as per chicken
	Steaks (Chateaubriand)	4 × 2 cm, slices at slight angle
	Best End	Slices, one with bone, one without
	Loins	As best end
	Legs	Hold knuckle, carve into bone
	Saddle	Traditional French: bone, cut in long slices; Traditional English: slice across grain
	Ham	As for leg, using long thin knife
Cooking meats	Steak Diane	Sauté, keep hot, onion, brandy flambé, cream, lemon, mushrooms
	Steak au poivre	Coat milled black pepper, sauté, (consommé, brandy, white wine)
	Boeuf Strogonoff	Strips, sauté, keep hot, onion, white wine, cream, rice served separately (mushrooms, tomatoes, chutney, vinegar)
	Monkey Gland Steak	Sauté, onion, Worcestershire sauce, brandy flambé
	Veal Escalope Smitane	See Steak Diane
	Veal Escalope Elizabeth Marie	Garlic, sauté, sherry flambé, bacardi, cream, asparagus
	Piccata Marsala	Sauté, keep hot, jus lié, marsala, monter au beurre
	Pork Escalopes	As above
	Chicken Supremes	As above
	Gammon (Highland Ham)	Pre-cook, whisky flambé, white wine, cream, tomatoes
	Offal (kidneys)	As per Steak Diane
	Kidneys au Madere	
Salads	Make up salads	Dressings: vinaigrette, mayonnaise, sour cream; Toss with dressing
Sweets	Crepes Suzette	Pre-cook, re-heat, orange, butter, sugar, curagao, brandy flambé
	Crepes Surprises	Ice cream in crepe, sauced, flambé
	Omelettes e.g. au Rhum	Can cook, sprinkle, spirit flambé
	Poached fruit	Reduce syrup, flambé
	Bananes au Rhum	Halve, butter, sugar, rum flambé
	Apples, pears	Fork on end to peel, halve, core and reform
	Oranges	On fork to peel, cut slices, squeeze end, sugar top
	Pineapple	Slice, cut out centre, sugar
	Grapes	Use grape scissors
Coffee	Small cona or filter	
	Turkish	Special grind, in ibrik (sugar), bring to boil three times, serve in demi-tasse
	Irish Coffee	Brown sugar in goblet, whisky, float double cream

Figure 2.10   (cont'd)

Preparation task	Mon. Lunch	Tues. Lunch	Wed. Lunch	Thurs. Lunch	Fri. Lunch
Check on Bookings – Reception Menu – Chef Staff – roster **Check equipment** Chilled cabinet Coffee machine Water boiler Hotplates					
Check resources Tablecloths Napkins Waiters cloths Coffee, tea, Milk, sugar Mustards etc.					
Ensure cleanliness Room, equipment, items					
Prepare Area Arrange tables etc. Check lighting, heating, music, etc. **Service area** Hotplates Stillroom **Bar** Payment point Till – clear, rolls, float					
Check lay-up Cruet – polish all items Table numbers					
Prepare side-table Check pads Menus Salvers Spare cutlery Cups and saucers					
Supervisor's check					

Figure 2.11 *Food service preparation tasks*

Task	Method	Detail
Personal presentation	Wash hands	Complete appearance
Finish tables	Water	Turn up glasses
Greeting	Welcome Take coats	Smile, greet Ask if customer has booked
Seat	Escort to table	Assist
	Meet initial needs	Menus, drinks, butter, bread, water
Take order	Check pad Copy to kitchen Copy for billing	From host? Suggest, sell Write clearly Confirm – repeat order Change cover
Serve	Plated meals	From left, cold food first, ladies first Accompaniments? Are customers happy with everything?
Clear	Each course	All finished Make ready for next course Crumb down after main course
Serve	Coffee, etc.	From right, coffee with milk/cream?
Take payment	Check bill then present	To host, return to collect Or at till, take payment
Farewell	Assist return coats Wish them goodbye	Check for any forgotten items
Re-lay	Prepare for next customers	
Clear	Area Ready for next use	Till cleared, takings recorded and secure Food returned
Debrief with food preparation staff	Any problems, complaints, compliments	Plan for improvements

Figure 2.12 *Table service tasks*

The summary of table service tasks in Figure 2.12 can be used as a format for particular meal occasions, particularly when part-time staff are involved. It can be amended to suit a particular meal and then copied for all staff and run through during a briefing session. The summary could include the menu if there was little or no choice.

The service of food dishes requires that there should be available the appropriate special items and accompaniments to ensure the satisfaction of customers and display of professional competence (see Figure 2.13).

Dish	Items	Accompaniments	Comments
Hors d'oeuvres	Fish plate, fish or small knife and fork	Oil and vinegar cruet	Plated or from raviers on tray or trolley
Fruit cocktail	In glass or coupe, teaspoon	Sugar dredger	
Melon	Dessert spoon and fork	Sugar and ground ginger	Whole, half or segment
Half a grapefruit	In a coupe, grapefruit spoon	Sugar dredger	
Prawn, etc. cocktail	In glass or coupe, teaspoon and oyster fork	Brown bread and butter	
Oysters	Opened on ice, oyster fork, finger bowl	Brown bread and butter, black and cayenne pepper, chilli vinegar, tabasco sauce	Oyster knife used to open them
Smoked salmon	Fish plate, fish knife and fork	Brown bread and butter, pepper mill	Sliced thinly
Smoked mackerel or eel	Fish plate, fish knife and fork	Brown bread and butter, horseradish sauce, pepper mill	
Caviar	Caviar knife, fish plate	Blinis or toast, lemon, sieved cooked egg white and yolk, finely diced onion, chopped parsley	25 g, in pot on ice
Pâté	Fish plate, small knife and fork	Toast, butter, pepper mill	
Asparagus	On fish plate tilted on a fork, finger bowl, debris plate	Hot: melted butter or hollandaise sauce Cold: vinaigrette	
Clear soup (consommé)	Consommé cup and saucer, underliner, dessert spoon		
French onion soup	Soup plate, underliner, soup spoon		Might be in a petite marmite
Bouillabaisse (Mediterranean fish stew)	Soup plate, underliner, soup spoon, fish knife and fork		
Minestroni	Soup plate, underliner, soup spoon	Grated parmesan cheese, optional croutes	
Pasta	Soup plate, spoon and fork	Grated parmesan cheese	For spaghetti, etc. fork on right, spoon on left
Whitebait	Fish plate, fish knife and fork, finger bowl	Brown bread and butter, cayenne pepper	
Fried scampi	Fish plate, fish knife and fork	Tartare sauce	
Grilled fish	Fish plate, fish knife and fork	Béarnaise Sauce	
Poached salmon	Fish plate, fish knife and fork	Hollandaise sauce	
Cold salmon	Fish plate, fish knife and fork	Mayonnaise	

Figure 2.13 *Some dishes with their traditional accompaniments*

Dish	Items	Accompaniments	Comments
Roast lamb	Main course plate, main knife and fork	Roast gravy, mint sauce	From carving trolley
Roast pork	Main course plate, main knife and fork	Roast gravy, apple sauce, sage and onion stuffing	From carving trolley
Roast chicken	Main course plate, main knife and fork	Roast gravy, bread sauce, lemon and thyme stuffing, bacon?	Carved at table
Roast turkey	Main course plate, main knife and fork	Roast gravy, cranberry sauce, chestnut stuffing	From carving trolley
Roast duck	Main course plate, main knife and fork	Roast gravy, apple sauce, sage and onion stuffing	Carved at table
Boiled salt beef	Main course plate, main knife and fork		From carving trolley
Roast game (feathered birds)	Main course plate, main knife and fork	Roast gravy, bread sauce, fried breadcrumbs/croutons	Whole?
Game (furred): venison, hare, boar	Main course plate, main knife and fork	Roast gravy, redcurrant jelly	From carving trolley
Salads	Half moon plates or bowls, small fork	Dressings: French, mayonnaise, soured cream	Dressed at table
Baked potatoes	Side plate, small fork	Butter pat	
Sweets	Dessert plate, dessert spoon and fork	Pouring cream from jug, sugar dredger for fruit or batter	
Cheeseboard	Dessert plate, small knife and fork	Crackers, butter, salt, celery	From cheeseboard with cheese knife
Dessert	Dessert plate, small knife and fork	Pouring cream from jug, sugar dredger, Kirsch	From fruit basket, grape scissors?
Coffee	Demi-tasse, saucer, underliner, teaspoon	Cream/warm, milk, sugar crystals, petits fours	Cafetière or from pots

Figure 2.13 *Some dishes with their traditional accompaniments*

Function catering

Traditionally called banqueting, function catering is the provision of services to a pre-arranged group of customers.

The occasions are very varied and may involve:

☢ **family – weddings, anniversaries**

☢ **business – conferences, exhibitions**

☢ **clubs and societies – dinners**

Figure 2.14 *Reception in a function suite*
Courtesy of The Grand Hotel, Brighton

Function catering is used at a variety of events including:

- ✪ **meetings, which require suitable seating arrangements, a table, paper, pencils, a jug of water and glasses**
- ✪ **exhibitions, which require access, display boards**
- ✪ **interviews, which require separate rooms, waiting space**
- ✪ **receptions, which can include any of the following: drink and beverages with simple finger foods, champagne with smoked salmon sandwiches, an informal meal, fork items, a full selection of cold prepared foods; these will require either space for a buffet table and movement of guests, or tables and chairs for all guests**
- ✪ **seated banquets with a simultaneous meal service – traditionally 'silver' service – a set menu and, if formal, speeches and a toastmaster**

This sector of catering is undertaken by virtually all catering enterprises but hotels tend to devote specialist accommodation to this purpose. There are also specialist concerns that work only in this field, such as the Connaught Rooms in London. Function catering is either carried out in house, or outside catering provides catering at other premises. Again outside catering is often done in a small way by all caterers with specialist firms for the large events.

The important factors in function catering are planning and organizing. The operations should be profitable, enhance reputation and provide varied and interesting work.

Figure 2.15 *Banquet layout*
Courtesy of The Grand Hotel, Brighton

The target market needs to be carefully considered, particularly the following factors:

- ✪ **facilities – rooms, amenities**
- ✪ **location – potential customers**
- ✪ **number of customers – limits set by safety criteria**
- ✪ **price and quality – appropriate to market conditions**
- ✪ **complexity – capability of staff and availability of materials and equipment.**

Publicity material should be produced in an attractive, understandable and accurate format for distribution to potential customers. The material should include:

- ✪ **plans of rooms with maximum numbers for different styles of event**
- ✪ **specimen menus and other services available**
- ✪ **description of the facility with easy to follow directions to find it**

Organization of function catering

A form is needed to record all the details of each function. This could be produced on a computer system or manually as in Figure 2.16. There will

Function..........................

Organizer Name	Date _ _ / _ _ / _ _ **Time** Set up Service Close
Position	**Type of function**
Address	**Numbers** Expected Advised Actual
Tel no.	**Menu**
Price **Payment method**	
Special requirements	
Printing menus, place cards	
Decoration flowers	
Staff toastmaster, photographer, porters	
Entertainment band, disco, cabaret	**Bar** Cash yes/no
Staffing	**Wines**
Equipment screens, projectors	**Table plan** Top table, rounds, dancing, buffet
Booking taken by **Date** .... _ _ / _ _ / _ _ **Manager responsible**	**Set up by** **Cleared by**
Remarks	

Figure 2.16 *Function sheet*

need to be copies of this form available for the different parts of the operation. It might also be used as the basis for a document which the organizer of the function signs to confirm the contractual relationship.

Traditionally in a hotel a banqueting manager would consult with the organizer and oversee the complete operation. Other staff involved are:

✪ **the chef, who will order the food and plan the preparation and cooking into the work schedule of the kitchen**

- **the head waiter/service supervisor, who will need to roster service staff who are often part-time employees from an agency or students**
- **the head barman and wine waiter, who will ensure supplies of drink are available and trustworthy staff are on hand to handle the valuable stock**
- **the head porter, who will move equipment and furniture**
- **the housekeeper, who will ensure the cleanliness of areas and the supply of linen**
- **the receptionist, who will need to be aware of all activities in the establishment in order to answer any enquiries and give accurate information**

Outside catering

These are catering operations that are carried out at premises other than the caterers. The planning and organizing is complicated by the need to create a professional working environment in premises which are often not designed for such use. These will include private homes, public buildings, sports arenas, and frequently open spaces with no facilities at all.

The caterer needs to consider not only aspects of preparation, cooking and serving food and drink but also the requirements for:

- **access – for supplies and staff, parking**
- **basic services – drainage, water, electricity and gas**
- **security – particularly if bars are to be set up**
- **equipment – assessment of on-site facilities and the need for others; the use of mobile kitchens, which are self-contained, may have to be considered**

Equally important is contingency planning against possible problems – the tool kit is as necessary as the knife set.

Communication between restaurant and kitchen

Communication is of critical importance and must be accurate and understandable. Food service personnel need to communicate with both the kitchen and the cashier (see Figure 2.17). This can be achieved by a range of methods depending on the size and complexity of the outlet and the amount of technology used. Direct access is ideal in a small outlet where

Food service	Co-operation	Food preparation
Sales analysis Customer comments Equipment Skills	Menu development and planning Team training	Stocks Seasons Equipment Skills
Bookings	Briefing	Availability
Orders	Oral Written Computerized	Provision
Special requirements	Personal interaction	Unforeseen events
Staff and customer comments Takings	Post-service briefing Planning for improvements	Staff comments Stock usage

Figure 2.17   *Areas requiring co-operation between food service and preparation*

communication may be oral. But a record must be kept for control and tax purposes.

Traditional methods of checking and billing include:

✪ **duplicate – an order taken with a top copy for food and drink and a duplicate for billing**

✪ **triplicate – as duplicate but with an extra copy for the food server's reference**

✪ **check/bill – one copy is used as the bill and presented to the customer**

Computerized systems may also be used. Orders may be taken down manually but billing carried out by a computerized till. Alterratively the complete system may be computerized with a hand held input and a display in the kitchen or bar as appropriate. The bill will be assembled and any additional orders will automatically be added.

It is essential that food service personnel provide accurate and understandable information to the kitchen and bar and that the system is capable of control so that discrepancies do not occur.

Staffing: food and drink service

The following skills are required to supervise staff who are selling, presenting and serving customers with food and drink:

- ✪ organizational
    - forecasting – demand, timing
    - planning – ordering for menus, effective use of resources
    - organizing – equipment, staff, materials to achieve objectives of quality and profit (or cost control)
    - controlling – ingredients, timing
- ✪ motivational
    - leading other staff in providing quality
- ✪ presentational
    - preparing room and tables, bar or counter
    - selling aids – menus, wine lists, displays, etc.
    - serving the dishes appropriately and attractively
    - maintaining the appearance of the room and table, bar or counter
- ✪ personal
    - taking pride in personal appearance with correct and clean uniform
    - taking pleasure in looking after customers, smiling and being be friendly, but not familiar or servile
    - balancing needs and wants of customers and organization
    - selling food and drink and other services and products
    - communicating effectively in writing and orally
- ✪ practical
    - preparing the area and table, counter or bar
    - clearing and relaying tables
    - taking and recording the orders
    - carrying, presenting and serving food and drink

These will need to be backed up with knowledge of the establishment's procedures and of the legal responsibilities, particularly as regards health, safety and hygiene.

Staffing structure

Clearly underlying all the previous factors is the appropriate combination of the number and quality of staffing involved in the food and drink service. Here are some widely required staff roles together with the appropriate qualification needed.

- ✪ **Restaurant manager**: This is the head of the staff in a large operation. The restaurant manager undertakes management, planning, organizing and controlling. He or she might be responsible to the food and beverage manager or might report direct to the general manager. (NVQ 4, HND or AGNVQ)

✪ **Supervisor, head waiter/ress (*maître d'hôtel*)**: The leader of the working team reports to the restaurant manager and is responsible for organizing, leading, co-ordinating and controlling the work of staff. The supervisor works in the restaurant and undertakes some practical activities such as supervising and leading the team, and checking for quality as well as quantity. (NVQ 3 or AGNVQ)

✪ **Wine waiter/ress (*sommelier*/butler)**: The wine waiter is a skilled operative who conducts the sale and service of drinks to customers at their tables. (NVQ 2/3, CG 707/2/3, Wine and Spirits Higher Certificate or equivalent)

✪ **Barperson**: The barperson sells and serves drinks from behind a bar. (NVQ 2/3, UKBG)

✪ **Assistant/commis**: A trainee or part-time member of staff traditionally assists the waiter/ress. (NVQ 1/2, CG 707/1)

✪ **Washer up/cleaners**: These staff are employed to clean and to wash up, etc. (Basic Hygiene Certificate)

Legislative requirements

Food and drink service systems must comply with health and safety, food safety and liquor licensing regulations. Figure 2.18 is a summary of the legislation which needs to be taken into account when preparing and serving food and drink. (See also Unit 5.)

Law	Description	Detail	Enforcement
Health & Safety at Work Act 1974	Makes all in a workplace responsible for health and safety	Provide safe premises, establish health and safety policy and safety committee	The Health & Safety Executive
Management	Risk assessment, Control hazardous substances	Training	Safety officers inspections, Environmental Health Officers (EHOs)
Workplace	Ensure floors have suitable finish and are easy to clean, Keep free from hazards	Supervision	
Manual handling	Lifting and moving heavy items	Training	
Fire precautions	Means to fight fires, Escape routes, Notices	Maintenance, Training, Fire precautions	Fire Service
Equipment, Dangerous machines	All should be safe and maintained, Electric slicing, mixing and cutting machines	Training, Must be over 18 and trained to use	Safety officers' inspections
Food Safety Act	Covers all premises, Training, Due diligence	Increase powers for EHO, Training, Use best practice	Safety officers' inspections, Environmental Health Officers
Temperature regulations	Keep food out of danger zone	Temperature control, Max. for chilled foods: 5°C, Min. for hot foods: 64°C, Reheat should be to 72°C	Safety officers inspections, Environmental Health Officers
Trade Descriptions Labelling Regulations	Criminal offence to sell food with a false description, Restrictions on use of fresh milk, etc.	Accurate measures and descriptions, GM foods or nuts present?	Trading Standards Officer
Price Marking Order	Display price of food and drink at entry to establishment including VAT		Trading Standards Officer
Weights & Measures	Food as well as drink	Testing of scales and measures	Weights and Measures Officer/TSO
Contract Law	Enforcement of agreements	Offer–acceptance–consideration	Courts
Licensing Acts	Sale and service of intoxicating liquor	Type of licence, age limitations, hours	Police, licensing magistrates
Customs and Excise	Alcoholic drinks at correct alcohol level	Training, supervision, equipment	Customs and Excise Officers

Figure 2.18 *Summary of legislation affecting food preparation and service*

Revision questions

1   Which combination of food and drink types would you be most likely to find in a fast food outlet?

(a)   Hot snacks, cold meals, alcoholic drinks
(b)   Cold meals, soft drinks, hot drinks
(c)   Soft drinks, hot meals, alcoholic drinks
(d)   Hot meals, soft cold drinks, hot drinks
                                              (2 marks)

2   Which option best describes a food court?

(a)   An open courtyard in the middle of a hotel with a barbecue
(b)   A number of different styles of food outlet with a common seating area
(c)   A restaurant with tables set out on a patio around a swimming pool
(d)   A collection of specialist food shops without seating   (2 marks)

3   Where is self-service the most likely method of food provision?

(a)   To hospital patients and for room service in hotels
(b)   For lounge service and in a hotel restaurant
(c)   In conference centres and school dining rooms
(d)   In a residential home and in aircraft
                                              (2 marks)

4   Which is always a feature of take-away service?

(a)   Home delivery service
(b)   Characteristic of fast food catering

(c)   Suitable for ethnic meals
(d)   Consumption away from the premises
                                              (2 marks)

5   Which outlet is likely to operate a silver service?

(a)   Directors' dining room
(b)   Food court
(c)   Public house
(d)   Sandwich bar   (2 marks)

6   What are likely to be the main objectives of food production in a hospital?

(a)   Nutrition and quality
(b)   Speed and nutrition
(c)   Quality and presentation
(d)   Presentation and speed   (2 marks)

7   What are the main objectives of food production in a motorway cafe?

(a)   Quality, product development, cost
(b)   Speed, product development, cost
(c)   Speed, consistency, quality
(d)   Product development, consistency, speed   (2 marks)

8   Food preparation must be organized efficiently. When planning work, which dish is started first?

(a)   The dish which is likely to sell most
(b)   The dish which requires preparation by several staff
(c)   The dish which requires most preparation and cooking
(d)   The dish which requires the most ingredients   (2 marks)

Keys to attainment

These are key skills or aspects of key skills that are central to the Food and Drink Operations unit. The key to attainment shows that the relevant aspect of the key skill has also been achieved. You will of course need to develop and practise the key skill during your lessons and in your private studies.

Communication, level 3

When you are:	You should have achieved the following key skills evidence:
Identifying and using relevant information for your investigation	C3.2 Read and synthesize information from two extended documents about a complex subject. One of these documents should include at least one image.
Presenting the results of your investigations	C3.3 Write two different types of documents about complex subjects. One piece of writing should be an extended document and include at least one image.

Signposts

These are naturally occurring opportunities for the development of key skills through your learning and assessment. You will not necessarily achieve the signposted key skill through your evidence for the Food and Drink Operations unit. You will need to develop additional evidence elsewhere to ensure that you meet the requirements of the key skills units fully.

Communication, level 3

When you are:	There may be opportunities for you to develop the following key skills evidence:
Talking to staff in outlets when investigating operations and observing staff at work	C3.1a Contribute to a group discussion about a complex subject.

Information Technology, level 3

When you are:	There may be opportunities for you to develop the following key skills evidence:
Presenting the results of your investigations	IT 3.2 Explore, develop and exchange information and derive new information to meet two different purposes. IT 3.3 Present information from different sources for two different purposes and audiences. Include at least one example of text, one example of images and one example of numbers.

Accommodation and front office

3

This unit explores the role of accommodation and front office operations within different types of hospitality outlets.

In this unit you will learn:

- **about accommodation and front office services in residential and non-residential outlets**

- **about the services accommodation operations provide for customers**

- **about the services front office operations provide for customers**

- **about the connection between accommodation, front office and the customer**

- **about the trends and developments within accommodation and front office operations**

Accommodation services

There are several types of accommodation within the hotel and catering industry:

- **sleeping (bedrooms, bathrooms)**
- **eating (restaurants, bars)**
- **circulation (halls, lobbies, lifts, stairs)**
- **meeting (syndicate rooms, board rooms)**
- **conference (halls, lecture theatres)**

All of these types of accommodation could be found in a large hotel (residential) although the majority occur in non-residential establishments.

The types of accommodation services provided in each establishment will vary according to the purpose of the establishment and the customer requirements. These could include:

- **cleaning**
- **valeting**
- **linen and laundry service**
- **service of food and drink**
- **conference services (for example audio-visual equipment, room layout)**

These services are tailored to meet the requirements of the customers.

One of the essential requirements is the need for security – both for customers and for their belongings. Customers have to feel that they are secure. This is a basic instinct that can be easily met by having, for example, locks, chains and/or peepholes on bedroom doors, clearly presented fire precaution instructions, good lighting, etc.

Other customer requirements might include various leisure activities provided within the establishment. Swimming pools, saunas, badminton and squash courts, fitness centres, etc. are frequently provided in both residential and non-residential settings. A wide range of back-up services for such leisure activities will then be required, including specialist staff in many cases.

Conference centres and other establishments providing business facilities (conferences, etc) will require a range of telecommunication facilities and services – telephones, fax machines, internet links, ISDN lines, overhead projectors, display screens, etc.

Customers may have a variety of individual needs and requirements which should be met wherever possible. Examples of such special requests can include a bed-board to produce a firmer bed, foam pillows in place of feather pillows to reduce allergic reactions and blankets instead of duvets.

Many of these requests can be ascertained before the guest arrives. For example, when taking the reservation, the receptionist should check if there are likely to be any special requests. It is obviously easier for the housekeeper to respond to such needs if they are identified in advance so that a response can be planned.

Types of provision

The types of provision found in an establishment could include aspects of the following categories, depending on customer requirements:

- ✪ **furniture**
- ✪ **fittings**
- ✪ **building security**
- ✪ **fire prevention**
- ✪ **lighting**
- ✪ **maintenance**
- ✪ **cleaning**
- ✪ **environmental considerations**

We now briefly review each of these provisions in turn.

Furniture

Furniture can be either fixed or free-standing. The design of the furniture should be suitable for the anticipated uses and furniture should display the British Standard Kitemark.

The choice of materials will be influenced by the purpose of the furniture and the type of room in which it is to be used. For example, in a hospital the furniture should be made of materials which can be kept scrupulously clean. In a luxury hotel bedroom, deep plush upholstery will often be appropriate. Space-saving furniture (for example folding doors, table extensions and leaves, foldaway beds) can be used where space is restricted. The more versatile the furniture, the more uses the accommodation can be put to.

Fittings

Fittings are generally taken to be items which are fitted or temporarily fixed to walls, for example paintings, pictures, mirrors, curtain rails.

Building security

Housekeeping staff are often on duty very early in the morning when there are few other people around. The staff need to have keys to gain access to store areas, offices, meeting rooms, etc. It is therefore essential that the staff are aware of security issues from the first day of their employment. Some of these issues are:

- ✪ **the security and care of keys**
- ✪ **the importance of unlocking rooms for cleaning and of securing them before moving on to other rooms**
- ✪ **the care of personal property belonging to the building's occupants**
- ✪ **the care of their own property**
- ✪ **the care and security of materials and equipment**
- ✪ **the need for vigilance and reporting of unauthorized personnel in any area**
- ✪ **the immediate reporting of faulty locks**
- ✪ **the immediate reporting of breakages or losses**
- ✪ **confidentiality of papers and documents**
- ✪ **the importance of checking the authorization of all people requesting access to rooms, for example workmen, guests who claim to have lost their keys**

Fire prevention

Fires can occur in any establishment and lives could easily be lost if rules are not followed. The Fire Precautions Act 1971 sets down regulations covering safety precautions in public buildings. For more detailed information, refer to the Fire Precautions Act. Some of the main points of the Act are listed here:

- ✪ **Fire doors are installed to prevent fire spreading around the building and should never be wedged open.**
- ✪ **Emergency exits should be kept clear at all times. Adjacent areas should not be used for storage.**

Area	Type of lighting
Lounge	Flexible for varying types of activity, e.g. reading, writing, small meetings, receptions
Reception	Maximum visibility for front office staff but foyer needs to be restful, quiet and welcoming for guests
Restaurant and bars	Good lighting needed for preparation and breakfast times More intimate background lighting needed for evening meals Spot lights or wall lights often used
Kitchen	Maximum visibility essential – fluorescent lighting most suitable
Bedrooms	Background lighting can be decorative, with additional lighting, e.g. on bedside tables, above mirrors, in study areas
Stairways and hallways	These must be well lit so there are no shadows Lighting from the ceiling will emphasize the edge of stairs and tread of each step On staircases, two-way lighting is essential In all hours of darkness the staircases should be lit to ensure safety

Figure 3.1 *Lighting requirements in different areas within an establishment*

- ✪ **Outside fire escapes should be well maintained and be well lit at all times. There should be nothing stacked on the escape or around the base.**
- ✪ **Lifts must never be used after a fire warning has been heard. The lift shaft can create a tunnel of flame, which easily spreads the fire to other floors if the doors are opened.**

Every establishment will have its own emergency procedures for dealing with fires and bomb threats. Fire procedures should be clearly written and a copy attached to each bedroom door. Staff must be trained in evacuation procedures.

Lighting

Lighting can make a difference to the atmosphere and comfort of a room. However, the safety of the room must always be a priority when choosing a lighting system. Figure 3.1 Shows the types of lighting suitable for use in a range of areas.

Maintenance

Maintenance can be broken down into two main sections: preventative maintenance and regular or routine maintenance. Both are essential to the smooth running of any establishment.

Preventative maintenance

This involves the regular care of fixtures and fittings on the premises, both internally and externally. As soon as a potential fault is identified, it must be dealt with in the appropriate way, thereby minimizing the potential disruption caused by the fault. Preventative maintenance is the responsibility of all members of staff in all types of establishment.

In the housekeeping department, areas of preventative maintenance can include:

- **plumbing – dripping taps, baths or sinks slow to clear, blocked overflows**
- **floors – frayed carpets, stains, bare patches**
- **windows – broken panes, broken catches, broken sashes**
- **doors – faulty locks, loose knobs, door catching on floor**
- **furniture – chipped, stained, shelves warped, loose screws and fitments**
- **fittings – curtain rails loose, pictures or mirrors unsteady**
- **electrical – loose light fittings, flickering lights**
- **equipment – not working efficiently, unreliable, noisy, frayed flex**
- **decorations – paintwork or wallpaper marked, chipped or torn**

Any faults should be reported to the duty housekeeper who would then report the fault to the maintenance department or contact a contractor for repair.

Regular maintenance

A complete check is made of every item in a given area at regular intervals. The housekeeper will instruct floor supervisors to carry out the checks in a quiet period. Any faults are recorded on a checklist. The housekeeper then collates the information and asks the maintenance department to carry out the identified repairs.

Establishments which are not open for 52 weeks of the year can carry out their regular maintenance checks and general maintenance when the establishment is closed.

The Greenalls Group

ENVIRONMENTAL

The Greenalls Group recognises that an active interest, involvement in and commitment to environmental issues is an essential part of business today.

To this end the Group is working to achieve best practice in the following areas:–

To conserve energy and other natural resources used in our operations

To keep emissions of gases into the atmosphere to the lowest practicable level

To minimise waste and effluent from our outlets and ensure that it is treated effectively before disposal

To work with our suppliers to keep packaging to a minimum, consistent with protecting the safety, quality and condition of products, and to use recyclable materials whenever possible

To ensure that in the building of and alteration to premises, due consideration is given to the use of low energy devices and renewable resources wherever practicable

To ensure that all Divisions of the group develop their own appropriate environmental policies within the framework of Group policy, and maintain adequate audit procedures to monitor compliance.

Appropriate training and resources will be made available as necessary to implement the above policy.

Signed

Chairman

Figure 3.2 *Environmental policy of the Greenalls Group*
Courtesy of the Greenalls Group

Environmental considerations

Most establishments have an environmental policy or statement which demonstrates their commitment to ensuring they carry out their business activities in the most environmentally-friendly way possible. An example of the environmental policy used by The Greenalls Group is shown in Figure 3.2.

Maximization of accommodation usage and revenue income

In order to maximize the accommodation usage and subsequent revenue income, it is essential that all areas of an establishment can be serviced and returned to their original state in an efficient manner and as quickly as possible. A housekeeper may need to review staffing levels and hours of work in order to ensure that all rooms can be serviced. It may be possible to let a bedroom in a hotel twice in a 24-hour period, for example as a day-let from 11am to 6pm and as a night-let from 9pm to 8am. This would only be possible if the room can be serviced between 6pm and 9pm.

A hotel housekeeper may use housekeeper's reports which can be produced for each section or station in the hotel (see Figure 3.3 on page 80). By using the information contained in the report, the housekeeper can plan the work of the room assistants and the room assistant will use the report to provide information on the status of each room and what type of cleaning or service is needed. The room assistant will usually mark off each room as the cleaning is finished.

Physical resources required to provide accommodation services

Here we consider some important physical resources used in the provision of accommodation services.

Cleaning materials

When choosing cleaning agents, the following must be considered:

- **the type of material and surface to be cleaned**
- **the type(s) of equipment to be used**
- **the capabilities of the staff**
- **the unit size and type of container (for example bulk, aerosol, litre)**
- **the availability of agents, minimum order, cost and delivery schedules**
- **the compatibility of cleaning agents**
- **the time needed to use the agents effectively versus the time available**

There are five main types of cleaning agents; these are detailed in Figure 3.4.

Run date: 4/6/01
Run time: 3:42
Report date: 4/6/01

Housekeeper's report

Room Status Codes:
B — Blocked
CLN — Clean
D — Due Out
DTY — Dirty
INSP — Inspected
OCC — Occupied
VAC — Vacant

Housekeeper Station 9

Room status	Room Type/No	Roll away	# Gst	Arrival date	Depart date	Depart time	Specials	VIP	Guest name	Notes
BD OCC/DTY	S/323		1	3/6/01	4/6/01				Boyle, Mr D	
BD OCC/DTY	S/324		1	3/6/01	4/6/0				Bouve, Mr F	
VAC/CLN/INSP	D/325									
OCC/DTY	DD/326		1	3/6/01	5/6/01				Hay, Mr S	
B VAC/CLN/INSP	D/327									

Figure 3.3 *Housekeeper's report*

Type of agent	Uses
Neutral detergents	Common general purpose detergents, used for washing dishes, damp dusting and mopping, and for routine cleaning tasks
Alkali detergents	Are corrosive – used for heavy tasks like stripping floors Should not be used too often as surface damage can result Some contain abrasives and should not be used on surfaces like plastic baths
Acid cleaners	Used for cleaning toilets and removing stains on baths and hand basins Important to follow instructions carefully – never mix with other cleaning agents as the combination may produce harmful chemicals
Solvent based cleaners	Able to dissolve heavy deposits of grease and oil Used for removing wax from wooden floors, for dry cleaning and stain removal
Abrasive cleaners	Scouring cleaners in powder, paste, cream or liquid form Used for cleaning enamel and ceramic sanitary ware

Figure 3.4   *Types of cleaning agents and their uses*

Cleaning equipment

When choosing cleaning equipment, various points should be considered:

Economy

✪ **The cost of the equipment – whether to purchase or lease**

✪ **Additional tools needed**

✪ **Type and cost of cleaning agents needed**

✪ **Running costs**

✪ **Can equipment be used for more than one task?**

Efficiency

✪ **Size of area and type of surface**

✪ **Standard of desired finish**

Electrical	Manual
Floor polishing machines	Trolleys
Floor scrubbing machines	Dustpans
Floor spray extraction machines	Carpet sweepers
Dry suction cleaners	Dusters
Wet and dry suction cleaners	Cloths
High-speed floor cleaning machines	Buckets
High pressure washers	Wringer buckets
Floor suction sweepers	Wet floor mops
	Dust-control mops
	Brooms
	Brushes
	Spray bottles

Figure 3.5 *Types of cleaning equipment*

Departmental

✪ **Servicing and parts replacement arrangements**

✪ **Ease of maintenance**

✪ **Size of storage area required**

Staff

✪ **Amount of effort required to use the equipment**

✪ **Size and weight of equipment**

✪ **Type of controls**

✪ **Ease of use**

✪ **Training needs for staff to use the equipment**

✪ **Safety of the equipment and operator**

The manager will have to consider how long the piece of equipment will last (its life expectancy) and if it will replace other cleaning processes and thus reduce cleaning time and consequently save money.

There are many different pieces of cleaning equipment. They can be broadly grouped into two types: manual and electrical. Figure 3.5 shows the types of equipment commonly used; not every establishment will have the need for each piece of equipment.

Storage of materials and equipment

Storage facilities need to be of an adequate size for handling and storage of equipment and materials. Without effective storage, wastage and inefficiency may occur.

The main requirements for correct storage include the following:

✪ **Each item should be stored in a specific place**

✪ **Those items used most frequently should be easily accessible**

✪ **Stock should be stored in such a way that it can be used in rotation**

✪ **Details of date of receipt and shelf life for every new delivery should be recorded**

✪ **Storage areas should be secure and access controlled**

✪ **Storage areas must be well ventilated, well lit and free from dampness**

✪ **Flammable items should be stored under special conditions and away from other items**

✪ **Adequate shelving should be provided**

✪ **Equipment should be stored near to the work areas**

✪ **Equipment, tools and accessories should be colour coded to allow the tools to be used correctly**

✪ **One person should be responsible for issuing all stock**

Physical resources and practical skills

For each cleaning task, the most suitable piece(s) of equipment should be chosen (see Figure 3.6 on page 84).

Before using any floor machines, operators must be fully trained and should ensure that they know how to stop the machine quickly. Some machinery, in particular floor scrubbers and buffers, is very heavy and difficult to co-ordinate.

When using the machinery, great care must be taken to prevent accidents caused by trailing leads, overstretched leads, unmarked wet floors and overuse of solutions.

Cleaning frequencies

Some cleaning tasks are carried out daily, others less frequently. Figure 3.7, page 85, identifies the cleaning frequencies that could be used in any establishment.

Room servicing

The servicing of rooms should be carried out with the minimum of disruption to guests or patients. The same methods should always be used for each task

Task	Equipment	Areas for use	Method	Safety
Dry dusting	Dry, soft cloth and duster for horizontal dusting Dry, soft brush or small mop for vertical dusting	Fixtures and fittings which are varnished, polished, painted, laminated or of vinyl material	Dust highest areas first working down to lower levels Work in a clockwise direction around room	Keep duster or mop in contact with surface to prevent scattering of dust Bacteria live in dust – essential to wash equipment thoroughly after use
Damp dusting	Cotton cloth Hand-held spray bottle filled with weak germicidal solution Container for litter and refuse	Impervious furniture and fittings	Remove refuse, ashtrays, plants and ornaments Spray small quantity of solution on to the cloth, wipe surface in overlapping strokes Edges and sides should be wiped after tops	Use correct dilution of germicidal detergent to ensure maximum destruction of bacteria Empty and wash out spray bottle regularly Always spray the cloth, not the item to be cleaned Do not direct the spray towards people Wash and dry cloth after use
Dry mopping	Long-handled dust control mop, straight or scissor design Dustpan and brush Container for litter and refuse	Dry, even floor surfaces	Keep mop firmly on the floor Work mop in a methodical manner up and down the floor area Overlap strokes to ensure all dust is collected; pay attention to corners Collect litter with dustpan and brush	When not in use, stand mop upright to prevent accidents Remove mop head and suction clean after use When soiled, wash in germicidal detergent, rinse and dry before use
Damp/wet mopping	Wet floor warning notices Two-section wringer bucket, one section filled with hot detergent solution, one with hot water Two floor mops Soft-headed broom and dustpan Wet pick-up machine	Impervious surfaces – to remove light soiling	Remove furniture if possible Sweep the area Using one mop and hot detergent solution, wet or damp mop the first section of the floor; with second mop and clean water rinse the first section Continue with this process until the floor has been cleaned Use wet floor warning sign If the surface needs to be dry immediately, use a wet pick-up machine to dry one section at a time	Change water as needed Ensure correct dilution and type of detergent are suitable for type of floor covering Wear non-slip shoes Empty and clean buckets after use Rinse and dry mops
Dry suction cleaning	Small, stiff hand brush Suction cleaner with attachments (if required)	Smooth impervious surfaces which need to be free from dust particles, e.g. hospital floors, carpeted areas, upholstery items and curtains	Pick up any small items from floor (e.g. paper clips, rubber bands); brush corners with hand brush to remove fluff Using cleaner, work across floor surface in a methodical manner, keeping flex behind the machine Use attachments as required for cleaning upholstery and curtains	Check dust container is empty before use Ensure flex does not trail as this can cause accidents Empty dust container after use and store the cleaner correctly

Figure 3.6 *Characteristics of different cleaning tasks*

Daily	Weekly
Dry dusting	Wipe paintwork
Damp dusting	Wash windows
Dry suction	Wax wooden furniture
Damp mopping	High dust control

Extra cleaning: stripping of entire room, e.g. clean carpet, wash curtains

Figure 3.7 *Cleaning frequencies*

Figure 3.8 *Hotel bedroom*
Courtesy of The Grand Hotel, Brighton

to make sure that results meet consistent standards. The types of cleaning equipment and supplies used should be kept to a minimum to reduce costs and save time spent on maintaining equipment. Any jobs that cause dust should be done before vacuum cleaning, which is usually the last task. Soiled items and rubbish should also be removed before other cleaning work starts as they may carry bacteria.

Once a cleaning routine has been established, the standards are monitored by the housekeeper. Figure 3.9 on page 86 shows a checklist used by a housekeeper in a five-star hotel. Cleaning routines will vary according to the establishment and are usually written down so all staff can use the same routine and items are not forgotten.

1 Place trolley with cleaning equipment, fresh linen and room supplies outside the room
2 Pull back curtains and open windows to ventilate room
3 Remove any food trays, bar glasses, etc.
4 Empty ashtrays and waste bins, including those in the bathroom – ashtrays should be emptied into a metal bin to avoid fire risk
5 Flush toilet, put in alkali detergent or strong acid cleaner
6 Strip beds
7 Remove all soiled linen and place in dirty linen bag
8 Remake beds
9 Leave dust to settle in room and clean bathroom
10 Damp dust all furniture, making sure that nothing is missed by starting at the door and moving in one direction, dusting everything in contact with the wall and then everything in the centre of the room
11 Check and replace guest supplies
12 Close windows
13 Check all electrical fittings are working and report any that are not
14 Replace ashtrays and waste bins
15 Vacuum clean floor and (weekly) upholstered furniture
16 Check the room's overall appearance, straighten pictures and remove any smears on mirrors
17 Leave the room locked and let your supervisor know it has been cleaned

Figure 3.9 *Suggested cleaning routine for a hotel bedroom*

Figure 3.10 *En-suite hotel bathroom*
Courtesy of The Grand Hotel, Brighton

Bed making

The bed is the focal point of a bedroom and should always look neat. An unmade or badly made bed can make a room look untidy. There are several different ways of making beds. Establishments may also have an individual house style that is preferred.

Blankets, duvets and bedspreads are changed periodically in hotels. However, in hospitals blankets and bedspreads are always changed when a person is discharged to prevent the spread of infection.

When stripping the bed, the linen should be flapped about as little as possible as it will scatter dust and bacteria around the room. The sheets and blankets should be removed one at a time and folded. Blankets, duvets and bedspreads, which are not being laundered, should be folded and placed neatly but not on the floor. Dirty linen should be placed in a dirty linen container.

Work methods

Block cleaning

This method is used primarily in university halls of residence when all rooms are vacant at the same time and are located close together. These rooms are usually occupied by the same people for an entire year and have lockable cupboards for valuables. Sets of rooms are cleaned in sequence instead of the normal method where each room is cleaned on an individual basis. Block cleaning is a quicker method and ensures that all tasks are completed in each room.

Team cleaning (also known as functional cleaning)

This method is used in areas where specialist cleaning is required, e.g. in hospitals. A floor maintenance team will be given specific tasks to do. The workforce is divided into teams, each specializing in one type of work which it carries out throughout the establishment.

Individual cleaning

This method is primarily used in hotels where each room assistant has the responsibility for a section of rooms. The room assistant will work alone and carry out all the tasks in that section of rooms.

Monitoring checklist

Ward/Department ....

Date .... Time ....

Reviewer .... P/F – Pass/Fail

1 Floors
Litter/dust/fluff	P/F
Build up	P/F
Spillage	P/F
Vacuum	P/F
Damp mop	P/F
Buffing	P/F
Scrub off	P/F
Shampoo	P/F

2 Sanitary fittings
Hand basins/sinks	P/F
Baths	P/F
Soap/towel dispensers	P/F
Toilet seat/bowl	P/F
Brush & holders	P/F
Commodes/sanichairs	P/F
Bins	P/F
Mirrors	P/F

3 Fixtures & fittings
Bed lights/call units	P/F
Curtain rails	P/F
Radiators	P/F
Fire extinguishers	P/F
Work surfaces	P/F
Window ledges	P/F
Monkey poles	P/F
Beds/bed frames	P/F

4 Furniture
Bedside lockers	P/F
Trolleys/wheelchairs	P/F
Chairs/stools/tables	P/F
Desks/filing cabinets	P/F
Cupboards/bookcases	P/F
Overbed tables	P/F

5 High & low cleaning
Pipes	P/F
Ledges/beams/frames	P/F
Notice boards/frames	P/F
Cupboard/door tops	P/F

6 Paintwork & glass
Walls	P/F
Doors/frames	P/F
Light switches	P/F
Panels/partitions	P/F

7 Waste disposal
Bins/sack stands	P/F
Correct disposal	P/F
Correct colour	P/F
Glass disposal	P/F

8 Consumables
Toilet paper	P/F
Soap	P/F
Towels	P/F
Bin liners	P/F

9 Kitchens
Work surfaces	P/F
Trolleys	P/F
Fridge	P/F
Cooker	P/F
Microwave	P/F
Cupboards	P/F
Dishwasher	P/F
Crockery/cutlery	P/F

10 Equipment
Mops	P/F
Trolleys	P/F
Electrical equipment	P/F
Buckets	P/F

11 Non-nursing duties
Water jugs	P/F
Flowers	P/F
Patients' washbowls	P/F
Stores	P/F
Unblocking sinks	P/F
Lighting	P/F
Cubicle/window curtains	P/F
Meal service	P/F
Beverage service	P/F

Comments:

Figure 3.11 *Monitoring checklist*

Staffing structures

Establishments will have different staffing structures depending on the types of service being provided.

Hospitals

The domestic services department (DSD) in a hospital provides, organizes and controls an effective cleaning service for the entire hospital, including wards, offices, theatres, outpatients, reception areas, laboratories and staff facilities.

When working in the wards, the staff must be efficient, fast and quiet while disturbing the patients as little as possible. The staff working in these areas must be able to cope with working among sick people.

The domestic services manager (DSM) is the head of department and responsible for staffing, planning, controlling the work of the department, keeping records and organizing work for domestic supervisors or assistant DSMs. Assistant DSMs deputize for the DSM and may have responsibility for one large section of the work. The assistant DSMs will be responsible for planning, organizing and controlling the workload of the domestic supervisors.

Domestic supervisors (supervisory) are responsible for daily planning, organizing and controlling a group of domestic assistants. The domestic supervisors use a monitoring checklist for monitoring and controlling the work of the domestic assistants (see Figure 3.11).

Domestic assistants (operative) are responsible for carrying out various cleaning tasks. They may have work schedules similar to those in Figures 3.12 and 3.13 (page 91).

DOMESTIC SERVICES DEPARTMENT
Work schedule – Fleming Ward
Domestic Ward Orderly
(Working 7.30am–7.30pm, Monday to Sunday)

Daily tasks

Ward areas

1	Remove all waste and place for disposal
2	Replace waste sacks and bin liners where required (making sure that yellow bags are tagged)
3	Clean sinks/basins including tiled surrounds
4	Damp dust high and low level surfaces
5	Vacuum floor areas

Figure 3.12 *Work schedule of a domestic ward orderly (1)*

6   Damp mop floor areas
7   Check clean sinks/basins in the afternoon/evening
8   Clean patient lockers externally and internally on vacation or at the discretion of the nurse in charge
9   Check clean floors in the afternoon/evening

Sanitary areas

1   Remove all waste and place for disposal
2   Replace waste sacks and bin liners where required (making sure that yellow bags are tagged)
3   Clean waste containers
4   Damp dust high and low level surfaces
5   Replenish supplies
6   Vacuum floor areas
7   Damp mop floor areas
8   Check clean sinks/basins in the afternoon/evening
9   Check clean floors in the afternoon/evening

Sluice, treatment and clinical rooms

1   Remove all waste and place for disposal
2   Replace bin liners where necessary
3   Clean waste containers
4   Damp dust high and low level surfaces
5   Clean basins/sinks, taps and surrounds
6   Clean all furniture, fixtures and fittings
7   Replenish supplies
8   Vacuum floor areas
9   Damp mop floor areas
10 Check clean floor in the afternoon
11 Check refuse containers again in the evening

Offices

1   Remove all waste and place for disposal (daily)
2   Replace bin liners where necessary
3   Clean all furniture, fixtures and fittings
4   Damp dust high and low level surfaces
5   Vacuum floor areas
6   Damp mop floor areas
7   Clean basins/sinks, taps and surrounds
8   Replenish supplies

Weekly tasks

1   Remove marks from paintwork
2   Clean internal glass
3   Clean blinds, making sure slats and cords are clean and knot free
4   Machine burnish floors
5   Damp clean shower curtains

Figure 3.12   *(cont'd)*

DOMESTIC SERVICES DEPARTMENT
Work schedule – Fleming Ward
Domestic Ward Orderly
(Working 7.30am–7.30pm, Monday to Sunday)

Daily tasks

Meal and beverage service

1 Prepare and serve beverages
2 Collect and wash up crockery as required
3 Collect, wash, refill patients' water jugs and glasses (morning, afternoon and as required)
4 Distribute, collect and collate patients' menus morning and afternoon
5 Assist with the distribution of meals to patients
6 Collect meal trays, crockery, cutlery and wash up
7 Wash up bulk food trolley tins
8 Damp wipe food trolley

Kitchen

1 Damp mop floor following meal service
2 Wipe down work surfaces following meal service
3 Clean sinks and taps following meal service
4 Record temperature of refrigerator (if this rises above 8°C report to the estates department)
5 Remove all waste and place for disposal
6 Replace waste sacks and bin liners where required
7 Clean waste containers

Nursing support duties

1 Change water of old flowers; collect, wash, dry and store vases
2 Clean and store tidily patient washbowls (weekly)
3 Receive, check and put away all provisions and domestic stores (weekly)
4 Change and rehang cubicle and window curtains as requested

Weekly tasks

1 Defrost refrigerator and clean
2 Clean cooker
3 Remove marks from paintwork
4 Clean internal glass
5 Clean blinds making sure slats and cords are clean and knot free
6 Clean cupboard interiors

Monthly tasks

1 Machine scrub floor

Figure 3.13 *Work schedule of a domestic ward orderly (2)*

Hotels

Cleaning and domestic services are provided by the housekeeping department. The main aims of the department are to:

- **promote the comfort of the guest, staff and visitors**
- **provide cleaning, laundry and linen services efficiently and economically**
- **assist in the maintenance of the fabric of the building, including promoting safety and health**

The department provides many extra services, such as flower arrangements, babysitting and dry cleaning.

The executive housekeeper or head housekeeper is responsible for a number of assistant housekeepers. The principal duties include:

- **staffing**
- **planning**
- **organizing the work of the department**
- **supervising the assistant housekeepers**
- **controlling standards of work and budgets**
- **liaising with other departments**
- **preparation and keeping of records**

Assistants or floor housekeepers have responsibility for one area of the hotel and organize and supervise the work carried out in that area as delegated by the head housekeeper. The linen keeper reports to the head housekeeper and is responsible for the provision and control of all linen services, including bed and table linen, staff uniforms and soft furnishings. Room assistants are responsible for the servicing of guests rooms, usually a section of ten to fifteen rooms. Cleaners are responsible for the servicing of all public areas, offices and cloakroom areas.

Halls of residence

Cleaning, catering and maintenance of the grounds is usually the responsibility of a domestic bursar, but this varies from one establishment to another. The principal duties will be as for the head housekeeper but will also include control of kitchen staff, conference organization and control of gardening and maintenance staff.

Assistant bursars can deputize for the domestic bursar or can be given specific areas of responsibility. Domestic assistants are responsible for cleaning procedures. Porters are responsible for security, high cleaning and for moving heavy furniture.

Methods of organizing work

Various methods can be used for organizing work in a hospitality and catering establishment.

Teams

A team is a group of individuals working together towards a clearly defined goal or objective. The ideal team will be made up of individuals who are all committed to the task in hand and have been given the necessary resources to do the job properly. It will operate in an 'open' and democratic fashion where all ideas and concerns are shared by the members of the team. As well as having the necessary resources to operate effectively, the team must be given the authority to make its own decisions and commit resources. Finally, for a team to be wholly effective in its tasks, it must have the full support of the senior management within the organization.

The benefits of team operation

Effective teamwork brings benefits to both the organization which sets up the team and to the individual team members. Benefits to the organization will vary depending on its size, structure and culture but are likely to include:

- ✪ **increased sales** – a teamwork approach to selling holiday accommodation by telephone is likely to yield increased sales compared with the same activity carried out individually

- ✪ **a happier workforce** – teamwork allows individuals to work to their full potential and feel good about themselves and their work

- ✪ **increased efficiency** – an example of this could be that an effective team working in the information department of a national hotel will be able to handle more enquiries from customers

- ✪ **less staff conflict** – a team which is trained to take responsibility for its own work and decision making is likely to be better at resolving its own internal problems, thus saving valuable management time

- ✪ **increased loyalty** – teamwork instils a sense of loyalty and commitment into members of staff

- ✪ **reduced absenteeism** – staff who see themselves as valued members of a team are likely to be more content and take less time off work

- ✪ **a more creative workforce** – team members are more likely to come forward with ideas for improving work practices, reducing costs or increasing efficiency

A vital reason for establishing a team to carry out a task is that it will operate more efficiently. For example, three people who previously prepared meals in the fast food restaurant individually and were able to prepare ten meals each per hour would be expected to prepare more than three times ten meals per hour when working as team.

Many of the tasks carried out in hospitality and catering organizations can only be accomplished through the efforts of a team of people. Tasks such as staging a banquet for 150 guests are too large and complex to be left to a single individual, or to workers who neither communicate with each other nor work as part of a team; in many cases, a team approach is the only solution.

Hierarchical structures

The opposite to teamwork is a highly centralized system of command and control. Here there is a clear line of authority from persons who are superiors to persons who are subordinate. We call these **hierarchical structures** for organizing work.

Work schedules

Another approach in organizing work is to make extensive use of work schedules. Two examples of work schedules for cleaning a hospital ward can be seen in Figures 3.12 and 3.13 on pages 89–90 and 91.

Work schedules should give any cleaning personnel the precise information necessary to clean a given area, including the length of time that this cleaning should take, the cleaning equipment and agents to be used, and the correct sequence to be followed when carrying out the cleaning.

Job procedures and checklists

The precise manner in which the work is to be performed can be outlined in a job procedure or checklist of activities, for example Figure 3.11 on page 88 shows a checklist used by domestic services supervisors undertaking a ward inspection. When guided by these procedures, staff are more likely to prepare the room to the required standard for a future guest or patient.

Rating scores in evaluation

Job procedure checklists may specify a method for 'rating' the activity, i.e. giving some type of numerical score which can be used in an evaluation and in a comparison with other situations.

When a room is ready for occupation it should be checked by the assistant housekeeper or supervisor who should enter the room and close the door. The first impression the room creates is the most important. The supervisor

Area	Time	Mon 1st	Tue 2nd	Wed 3rd	Thurs 4th	Fri 5th	Sat 6th	Sun 7th
1	7am–3pm	Mary	Mary	Brenda	Brenda	Mary	Mary	Mary
2	7am–3pm	Kay	Kay	Kay	Kay	Brenda	Brenda	Kay
3	7am–3pm	Sue	Sue	Sue	Jane	Jane	Sue	Sue
4	2pm–10pm	Kate	Kate	Jane	Kate	Kate	Jane	Kate
5	2pm–10pm	Jane	Brenda	Doris	Doris	Doris	Doris	Doris
6	2pm–10pm	Joan	Joan	June	June	Joan	Joan	Joan

Figure 3.14 *Example of a rota*

should proceed slowly around the room in a clockwise direction looking high up first, then at eye level, then at table top level, then low down. All faults or soiled areas should be noted on a form, fed back to the room assistant, corrected and then rechecked.

Order-of-work cards

These are pocket-sized cards which detail the materials and methods to be used in a task. For example, in a cleaning task details of the cleaning equipment, agent and method of work for performing that specific task, such as cleaning a toilet or bath, may be on a printed card. Staff can carry these cards in a pocket for easy reference.

Duty rotas

Rotas or rosters are used to show hours of duty, area of work and days off. They are produced weekly or, where advance information is available, monthly. An example of a rota is shown in Figure 3.14.

Reasons for controlling work

It is necessary to monitor and control work in order to:

- ✪ **establish that quality and efficiency standards are being met**
- ✪ **ensure all operatives work to the same standards**
- ✪ **ensure all supervisors measure the same standards**
- ✪ **establish staff development needs**
- ✪ **motivate staff and improve morale**

✪ **ensure complete customer satisfaction**

✪ **reduce complaints**

Different types of establishment will have different reasons for controlling work but those listed above should be the minimum.

Budgetary controls

Like any other department, the housekeeping department is involved in the finance of the establishment. The costs in providing a housekeeping service must be established.

In housekeeping, the costs can generally be broken down as follows:

✪ **Direct**

- **Labour (housekeeping staff)**
- **Materials**
- **Electricity, gas**
- **Maintenance**

✪ **Indirect**

- **Labour (managers, reception, etc.)**
- **Rent, rates**
- **General administration**
- **Advertising**

The costs of providing a service can be calculated by adding all the direct costs involved in providing that service, for example servicing one bedroom. The indirect costs will be apportioned to the department.

Housekeeping staff can reduce costs by ensuring cleaning agents are not wasted and staff are correctly trained in the tasks they are expected to carry out.

Front office services

The reception and front office departments of any establishment are the first contact points for the majority of customers of the organization. This is where first and lasting impressions are made as regards the establishment, whether by direct contact in person, or by letter or telephone.

Figure 3.16 on page 98 indicates that there is logical cycle of events concerning the reception department starting with the initial enquiry. This reception cycle may involve a lengthy period of time, perhaps even years! The customer may make an enquiry about a reservation a couple of years in advance of the stay, for example when planning an international conference. After customers have checked out, they are not forgotten – they may be included in mailshots as part of marketing campaigns, and their opinions may be sought as to the operations of the establishment. At all stages in the cycle a high standard of service must be provided. This can be achieved by ensuring systems and procedures are standardized and followed by all members of staff. More information on customer service can be found in Unit 4.

Dealing with enquiries

People will approach the reception desk with a range of enquiries, some of which will be very important and/or urgent, while others will be simply

Figure 3.15 *The Grand Hotel, Brighton*
Courtesy of The Grand Hotel, Brighton

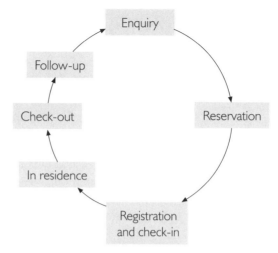

Figure 3.16 *Reception cycle*

general enquiries. It is impossible for a receptionist to know the answer to every question. However, it is reasonable to expect a receptionist to know where, or from whom, the information required can be readily obtained.

Product knowledge (knowledge of the establishment) is an essential requirement for a receptionist. Without product knowledge a receptionist will be inefficient and will not be competent or happy. It is very demoralizing to keep on answering questions with 'I don't know'.

Many establishments keep an up-to-date handbook containing information on procedures and policies as well as details on special offers and promotions and information on local attractions. By ensuring that this handbook is kept updated, the front office team will always have the information needed readily available.

All customers should be greeted promptly, with a smile. Any other people still waiting for attention should also be acknowledged. Once they appreciate that the receptionist realizes they are there, they will be happier to wait a little longer. Ignoring people at the desk only irritates them and makes matters worse. Customers' names should be used whenever possible. Customers then know that the receptionist is interested in them and they will feel more at ease.

The receptionist should listen to the person talking and ask questions to clarify the situation if necessary. Once the enquiry has been fully understood the receptionist should decide whether to deal with it directly or whether to involve another member of staff. The customer should always be told what is happening or who will deal with the enquiry.

Date	Surname	Forename(s)	Address	Signature	Nationality	Room no.
1.12.2000	Smith	Patrick	1 High Street Dover, Kent CT16 7AB	P. Smith	British	17

Figure 3.17 *Entry in a registration book*

Registration and check-in

When the customer is checking in, a registration process will need to be followed. Depending on the establishment, various procedures will have to be followed.

The Immigration (hotel records) Order 1972 stipulates the information that must be obtained from guests staying in a hotel. All customers over 16 must provide their full name, nationality and date of arrival. If customers are from overseas, they must also provide their passport number and place of issue, and their next destination and address.

Customers may register in a book (see Figure 3.17) or on individual cards (see Figure 3.18 on page 100), which is the system used by most hotels. Hotels also use this opportunity to obtain more information about guests. On the registration card shown in Figure 3.18, you can see that The Grand Hotel asks for the car registration number and method of payment. The hotel also enquires if the guest is a Club De Vere member and gives the guest the opportunity to decline to be sent information from the company.

The hotel asks for the car registration number for two main reasons. Firstly, if the guest parks the car on hotel property and the guest leaves the car lights on accidentally, the hotel can notify the owner; also, if there is any other problem with the vehicle, such as accidental damage, they can trace the owner. Secondly, should the guest leave the hotel without paying, the hotel can give this information to the police – though of course the guest may have given false car registration details!

THE GRAND HOTEL
WELCOMES

MR I T WELDON

GUEST VALUABLES may be deposited with Reception and a receipt obtained. May we also draw your attention to the Hotel Proprietors' Act 1956, which is displayed at Reception.

FIRE INSTRUCTIONS are displayed on your bedroom door, please familiarise yourself with them and your nearest fire exit.

CHECK OUT IS AT 11 a.m. Should you wish to keep your room after this time, please check with Reception.

PLEASE KEEP THIS CARD WITH YOU FOR IDENTIFICATION WHEN COLLECTING YOUR KEY OR CHARGING ITEMS TO YOUR ROOM.

ROOM No:- 511

ARRIVAL DATE:- 22/06/99

DEPARTURE DATE:- 23/06/99

RATE:-
24 HR CONFERENCE RATE
'SOLARIUM TREATMENTS'
007T TAN--£4.50, PHONE 2046

GUEST'S SIGNATURE

REGISTRATION CARD

Account No.	Arrival Date	Departure Date	Arrival Time	No. of Rooms	Room Type
485266	22/06/99	23/06/99	*GTD*	1	ZL INLAND

Rate	No. of Guests	Deposit	Room No.	Basis
	1		511	

EXAMPLE

Full Name Please Print

Home Address

Postcode | **Tel. No.**

Car Reg. No. | **Nationality**

Signature

If you do not wish to receive any further information from The Greenalls Group, please tick this box. ☐

Overseas Visitors
Passport No.
(No. du Passeport)
Issued at
(Delivre a)
Destination Address
(Addresse de Destination)

Method of Payment
Cash ☐ A/c to Company ☐
Cheque ☐ Credit card ☐

Are you a Club De Vere member?
No ☐ Yes Number

Figure 3.18 *Registration card*
Courtesy of The Grand Hotel, Brighton

The hotel asks about the method of payment in order that the appropriate credit worthiness checks can be made. If the guest is paying by cash, the hotel may ask for prior payment. If the guest is paying by cheque, the receptionist should remind the guest about the hotel's policy regarding accepting cheques (there may be a limit unless the hotel uses Transax or a similar system to obtain immediate clearance). If the guest is paying by credit card, the receptionist may ask to 'swipe' the card through the machine in order to obtain the card details prior to check-out. If the guest has ticked the 'A/c to Company' box, the receptionist must verify that the company has confirmed in writing that it will settle the account, and must also check exactly what the company will pay for. The hotel will probably have a credit policy and will have given a credit limit to the company.

In establishments using a computerized system, the registration cards are printed with the details of each individual guest before they arrive. The cards are usually printed off during the night. The card clearly shows all the guest details, which should of course be correct! To register, the guest just needs to

Figure 3.19 *Front part of the registration card shown in Figure 3.18*
Courtesy of The Grand Hotel, Brighton

check that the details are correct and then sign at the bottom. The top part of the card in Figure 3.18 is detachable and is used as a key card. The front part of this card is shown in Figure 3.19.

The registration information must be kept for 12 months and be made available for inspection by the police.

The customer is issued with a room key and the key card (Figure 3.19), which gives information on the hotel. The key card may also confirm the arrival date, departure date, room number and price of the room. It records the customer's name and signature.

In-house services

Check-in is an ideal time to promote the in-house services of an establishment. These will vary but generally include:

- ✪ **room service – menu**
- ✪ **customer relations**
- ✪ **portering service – luggage, car parking**
- ✪ **housekeeping service – laundry, dry cleaning**
- ✪ **office services – secretarial**
- ✪ **health and leisure services – leisure club, salons**
- ✪ **telephone message services**
- ✪ **information services**

Some establishments, hotels in particular, produce an in-house video, which is screened 24 hours a day on the television in bedrooms. This video will

The Manor Hotel
Westmouth Street, London WC2 8SP
Tel 0208-669-1111 Fax 0208-669-1416

Miss M Jones _____ Room No _25_

173 High Street, Harlow, Essex

DATE	3/6/1995						
Brought forward							
Apartment	71	00					
Breakfast							
Early morning tea/coffee							
Newspapers							
Telephone	6	20					
Paid out							
Laundry							
Sundries							
Lunch							
Dinner	16	50					
Wines & spirits	3	80					
DAILY TOTAL	97	50					
GRAND TOTAL	97	50					
Less cash							
Transfer to account							
Carried forward	97	50					

VISITORS ARE REQUESTED TO VACATE THEIR APARTMENTS
BY 12 NOON ON THE DAY OF DEPARTURE

ACCOUNTS DUE ON PRESENTATION   **PLEASE LEAVE YOUR KEY**

This VAT invoice will be completed on request

	£	p
Total Taxable Hotel Services (excl. VAT)		
Amount of VAT @ %		
Total Taxable Hotel Services (inc. VAT)		
Total Non-Taxable Items (exempt)		
Account Total		

VAT Reg. No. 239 5949 76

Figure 3.20   _Handwritten bill_

promote the restaurant, bars and leisure facilities, and encourage the use of the room's mini bar and pay-to-view videos.

Directories containing detailed information on in-house services are usually placed in a prominent place in bedrooms. Many establishments will also promote the services and facilities using framed posters, tent cards, leaflets and displays in public areas.

The in-house services must meet customer requirements, and be modified when and where necessary following customers' comments and market forces.

Billing procedures

While customers are in residence, billing procedures are followed to ensure that they are charged for all the services and facilities that they use. The billing system used varies in each establishment but the principles are the same.

The establishment and the customer need to know how much has been spent in each area, for example restaurant, bar, telephone or room, on a daily basis. This can be recorded manually using a tabular ledger and handwritten bill (see Figure 3.20). However, most establishments now use a computerized system, where some charges are automatically added to a customer's account using a terminal located at the point of sale. In some establishments details of charges for posting to guests' accounts are passed to the front office on dockets.

Whatever system is used, it is balanced daily and always kept up to date. A computerized print-out of the total bill is usually always available (see Figure 3.21).

Payment methods

There are various methods of payment that guests may wish to use. Not all establishments accept all types of payment, so it is important that anyone who deals with payments knows what is acceptable and how to handle it.

The main types of payment generally accepted are:

- **sterling cash**
- **foreign currency**
- **sterling cheques**
- **Eurocheques**
- **traveller's cheques**
- **credit cards**
- **charge cards**
- **debit cards**
- **vouchers**
- **ledger payments**

Cash

When accepting cash in the form of notes it is important to ensure that the money is genuine. Small ultra violet light units can be used to help detect forged notes. Cash must be treated with care and must be counted on

King's Road, Brighton, East Sussex, BN1 2FW Telephone: **01273 321188** Fax: 01273 202694

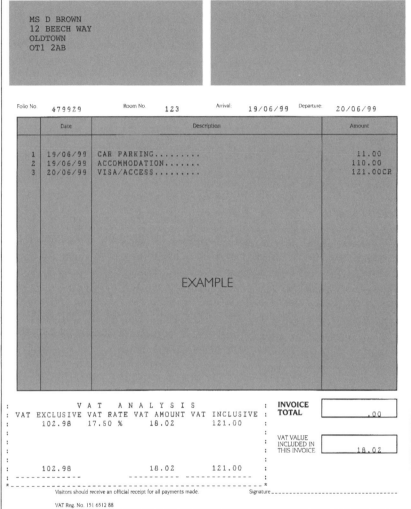

Figure 3.21 *Computerized print-out of a total bill*
Courtesy of The Grand Hotel, Brighton

acceptance, with change counted out to the customer and the customer's payment stored correctly.

Foreign currency

Some hotels will still change foreign currency into sterling as a service to their residents. These transactions normally take place outside normal banking hours. Other hotels will not change foreign currency into sterling but will accept foreign currency as a payment method for an account.

When changing foreign currency, it is essential for a cashier to know the exchange rates. These rates should be displayed and the customer must be advised of the exchange rate and commission charges before the exchange is made. Notes only are acceptable. Not all currencies can be changed.

Foreign currency is changed as follows: A customer gives the cashier 1000 French francs, for example. The rate for today is 8.05 francs for every pound. The cashier would divide 1000 by 8.05 to find out how many pounds sterling the customer should be given. The answer in this case is £124.22.

Some hotels charge a flat commission rate of say £5.00; others make a percentage commission charge. Customers must be given a receipt, which shows the currencies, amounts, exchange rate and commission charges.

Sterling cheques

Banks and building societies issue sterling cheques. A cheque guarantee card guarantees a cheque. The cards will guarantee a cheque up to a certain limit, starting at £50 and rising in multiples of £50. The amount guaranteed by any particular card is printed on the card. The bank guarantees payment of the cheque providing certain conditions are met. The **drawer** (the person whose account it is) must sign the cheque in view of the cashier. The **payee** (or the person accepting the cheque on behalf of the payee) then checks that the signature on the cheque matches that on the card, the card is for the same bank account as the cheque and the card is valid. The payee then writes the card number on the reverse of the cheque. The payee accepts only one cheque per transaction with the guaranteed limits. The cashier accepting the cheque must ensure that it has been dated correctly, that the amounts shown in words and figures agree and that the conditions have been met (see Figure 3.22).

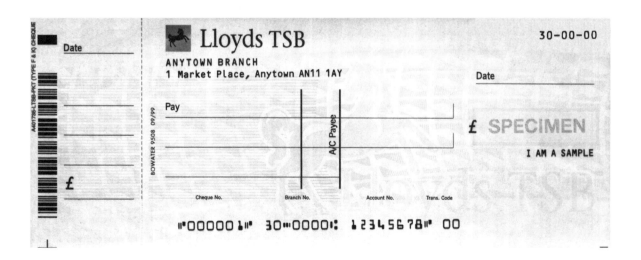

Figure 3.22   *Example of a blank sterling cheque*
Courtesy of Lloyds TSB Bank plc

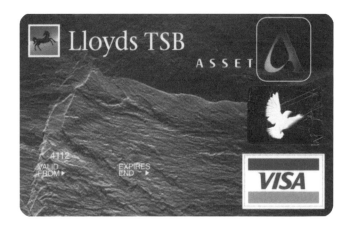

Figure 3.23 *Example of a Lloyds TSB Visa card*
Courtesy of Lloyds TSB Bank plc

Eurocheques

A Eurocheque is a cheque drawn on the customer's bank account which can be used anywhere within the EU. It is written in the currency of the country where the payment is being made. Eurocheques are slightly different from other cheques in that more than one cheque can be written out per transaction, and the guarantee card is valid only for one year, which runs from January to December.

Traveller's cheques

Customers will have paid for their traveller's cheques when they collected them from their bank or travel agency. Traveller's cheques are in fixed denominations and are issued in most currencies.

When accepting traveller's cheques, it is important to check the customer's identity, to watch the customer countersign the cheque and to write the customer's passport number or room number on the reverse of the cheque. Change can be given to the customer who uses traveller's cheques to settle an account. Traveller's cheques in foreign currency are treated as foreign currency, usually with an increased commission. Any change is given in sterling.

Credit cards, charge cards and debit cards

Visa and Mastercard are credit card brands, and are easily recognizable by their logos (see Figures 3.23 and 3.24).

American Express, Diners Club and Carte Blanche are internationally recognized charge cards. Some hotel companies also issue their own charge cards.

Debit Cards directly debit the customer's bank account with the total of the bill and place that amount in the establishment's bank account. Most common cards of this type are Switch, Delta and Connect cards.

Figure 3.24 *Example of a Lloyds TSB Mastercard*
Courtesy of Lloyds TSB Bank plc

Each establishment has a floor limit, which is the establishment's credit limit without authorization for non-cash payment. Its purpose is to reduce fraud. If the payment amount is above the floor limit, authorization can be sought from the issuing company. When authorization is given, the code must be written in the appropriate place on the sales voucher, otherwise the issuing company will not meet the payment. When accepting credit cards, it is important that the cashier makes the following checks:

✪ **Is the card valid? The start and expiry dates should be checked.**

✪ **Has the card been tampered with? If so, it should not be accepted.**

✪ **Has the card been signed?**

✪ **Is the amount below the floor limit? If not, authorization should be obtained.**

✪ **Is the card on the stop list?**

Some establishments use a manual method of processing credit card payments, using a credit card imprinter and sales vouchers.

Other establishments use a mechanized system. The process data quickly (PDQ) terminal is a hand-held battery operated unit where authorization is not automatic and transaction data is stored in the terminal on removable smart cards. Usually in the front office area, the terminal is larger and remains fixed on the desk. With this system, authorization can be requested automatically since the machine is linked via a telephone line to the company operating the system (usually Barclaycard Merchant Services).

Vouchers

Some customers may make a reservation through a travel agent and will pay the travel agent for their accommodation in advance. The travel agent will issue a voucher to the customer and to the hotel providing the service. On arrival at the hotel, the customer will give the voucher to the hotel. At the end of the stay, the hotel will submit an account to the travel agent requesting payment. It is important to note that not all vouchers issued by travel agents have monetary value; each voucher should be carefully checked to establish what it does cover.

Ledger payments

Some companies may request to have credit facilities with an establishment providing accommodation and/or meals, and/or conference facilities. Before a credit limit can be set, the company will have to provide information to enable their credit worthiness to be checked. The supplying establishment will, on receipt of this information, be able to decide if the requesting company can have credit facilities.

Once the facility is agreed, the company will be asked to confirm in writing each account it wishes to be sent to them for payment and to specify which charges it will settle. For example, will they pay for drinks from the bar or must the customer pay for these at the hotel/restaurant at the time of departure? Once an account has been sent to a customer for payment, a ledger account is established.

Check-out

When customers check out of the establishment, they settle any outstanding charges on their account. This is an excellent opportunity for the receptionist or cashier to check that the customer is satisfied and to promote the establishment, perhaps by offering to book another room in part of the 'chain'.

After departure, the customer is reminded of the time spent at the establishment and prompted to return by being sent revised brochures, details of speciality weekends and loyalty bonuses, etc.

Documentation

The reception department is able to produce for the establishment many documents and lists, both before guests arrive and when they are in residence.

Arrivals list

An arrivals list is an alphabetical list of guests expected to arrive on a particular day. The list is usually prepared one day in advance and can be circulated to

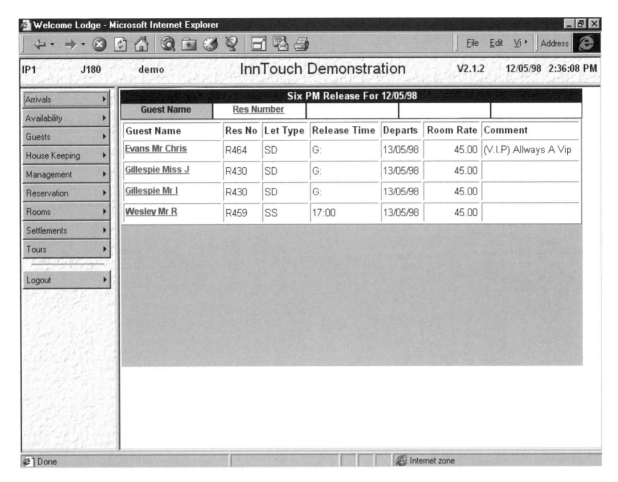

Figure 3.25 *Arrivals list*
Courtesy of Innsite Hotel Services Limited

the various hotel departments and management. It includes details concerning guest reservations such as room type, length of stay, room rate and account details. An example of an arrivals list is shown in Figure 3.25. In this example you can see that there are four expected arrivals. Three of the reservations are guaranteed and one has a 1700 hrs release time.

Departures list

A departures list gives information on guests who the hotel expects will depart from the hotel on that particular day.

Guest list

A guest list shows a list of guests currently staying (sometimes called residents) in the establishment.

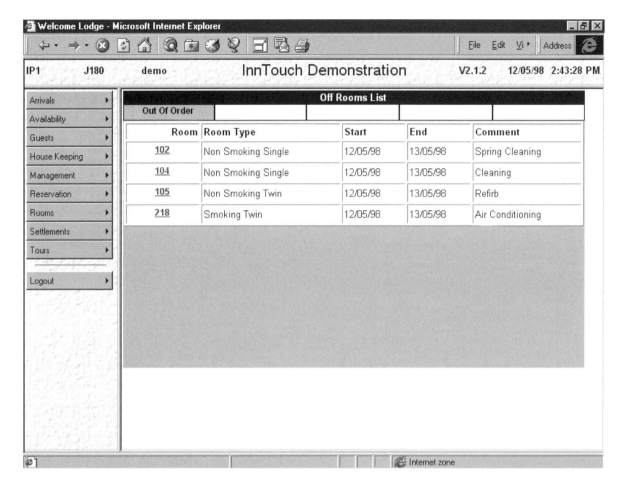

Figure 3.26 *Off rooms list*
Courtesy of Innsite Hotel Services Limited

Room status report

The room status report gives information on each room and shows whether the room is occupied or vacant, and whether it is ready for occupation or whether it has not yet been serviced and is still dirty. Some rooms may be shown as 'OOO' this means that they are 'out of order'. The room may be in the middle of redecoration or there may be a fault with the room, which prevents it from being 'sold'.

The room status report is updated as soon as a guest checks in or out and as soon as serviced rooms have been inspected by the housekeeper and are declared 'ready' for letting.

An 'off rooms' list shows details of all rooms which are not available for letting and gives the expected date that the room will be available again (see Figure 3.26).

Housekeeper's report

A housekeeper's report is generated in reception daily (or by the housekeeper if they have a PC and printer) and provides the housekeeper with a sectional list of rooms. Each section will contain a number of rooms.

From this report (see Figure 3.3, page 80) the housekeeping staff will know which rooms are vacant, which rooms are occupied (and for how many more nights), and which rooms are about to be vacated. They will then be able to service the rooms accordingly.

Sleeper forecast

A sleeper forecast is produced for a certain period of time in advance. In the example in Figure 3.27 on page 112 it is for the period 01/07/01 to 14/07/01. The forecast shows the expected numbers of departures, arrivals and sleepers for each day and gives a guide to the different departments for planning staffing levels, food ordering, etc.

The reservation system

Within the front of house areas, it is the reservations section that generates the most income and is therefore the most vital. Every establishment that reserves bed spaces will need to use a reservation system. The type and complexity of the system will depend upon the particular requirements of the establishment.

In this section you will be introduced to the most popular methods of recording reservations. Whichever system is operated, the same principles apply.

Room reservations

There are seven major methods of communicating a reservation request to a hotel:

- ✪ **telephone**
- ✪ **letter**
- ✪ **personal**
- ✪ **fax**
- ✪ **computer**
- ✪ **email**
- ✪ **internet**

In some instances reservation requests will combine more than one of these systems, for example a telephone booking which is then confirmed by letter. The system for processing these reservations does not differ significantly.

Sleeper forecast
01/07/01–14/07/01
Date & time of report: 25/06/01 15:35

	Departures			Arrivals			Sleepers		
Date	Rooms	People	Child	Rooms	People	Child	Rooms	People	Child
01/07/01	1	2	0	15	16	0	43	47	0
02/07/01	36	40	0	8	13	0	15	20	0
03/07/01	7	9	0	10	14	0	18	25	0
04/07/01	8	13	0	32	35	0	42	47	0
05/07/01	3	4	0	43	43	0	82	86	0
06/07/01	13	13	0	22	25	0	91	98	0
07/07/01	25	28	0	31	47	0	97	117	0
08/07/01	37	53	0	8	8	0	68	72	0
09/07/01	52	55	0	28	31	1	44	48	1
10/07/01	15	16	0	8	12	0	37	44	1
11/07/01	28	34	1	17	19	0	26	29	0
12/07/01	5	7	0	23	23	0	44	45	0
13/07/01	9	9	0	7	6	0	42	42	0
14/07/01	8	7	0	2	2	0	36	37	0
Totals	**247**	**290**	**1**	**254**	**294**	**1**	**685**	**757**	**2**

Figure 3.27 *Sleeper forecast*

Handling reservation enquiries

In order to demonstrate the hotel's efficiency, it is essential that all enquiries are handled promptly and correctly. A performance standard objective may be that every enquiry for accommodation is developed into a sale, thereby maximizing the hotel's occupancy and its revenue. The revenue gained from room sales accounts for the majority of a hotel's total revenue.

Figure 3.28 shows every possible combination of a reservation request. From this we can follow a telephone request (A) for a twin with bath on the 23rd of next month (B) for three nights through the diagram.

At point (C) the reservation clerk needs to decide which response to give to the client. The state of future bookings cannot be stored in the head of the

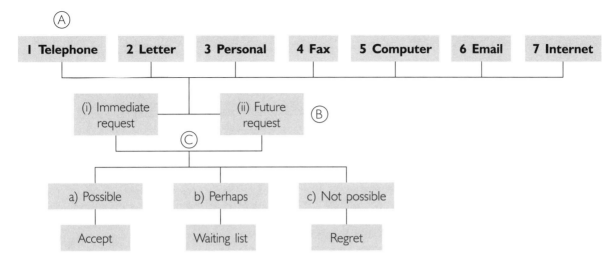

Figure 3.28 *Combinations of reservation requests*

reservation supervisor, so some form of recording system is required. It is the booking chart that the reservation clerk will refer to, in order to check whether or not the accommodation is available (establishments using computerized systems will use the reservations package on the front office system).

Assuming that the accommodation is available then the reservation clerk will need to record the relevant information. This is done most easily on a pre-printed reservation form (see Figure 3.29, page 114). The form acts as a checklist to ensure all the relevant information is obtained and as a reminder to tell the guest all the relevant information (price, etc.). It is less easily lost than a scrap of paper and is easier to process.

The details of bookings are transferred to a reservation diary from the reservation form. This diary is normally a loose-leaf book with one page per day. On the arrival day, this will serve as a basis for the production of an alphabetical arrivals list.

To handle a cancellation the same procedure is carried out in reverse, i.e. the booking is marked as cancelled in the diary and erased from the chart, and the correspondence is refiled.

Regardless of the method of approach the guest uses, the reservation clerk should always follow the same procedure. Before the reservation clerk can take a reservation, some essential information is needed from the guest:

- ✪ **date of arrival**
- ✪ **length of stay**
- ✪ **type of room required**
- ✪ **number of rooms required**

With this information, the reservation clerk can check the reservation records and determine if the reservation can be accepted. When using a

```
┌─────────────────────────────────────────────────────────────┐
│                     ROOM RESERVATION                          │
│  NAME.................................ARRIVAL DATE.............. │
│  ADDRESS...............................NO. OF NIGHTS........... │
│  CITY....................................PHONE................. │
│  SINGLE ☐   TWIN ☐   STUDIO ☐   NO. OF PERSONS.............. │
│  DOUBLE BED ☐   SUITE ☐   RATE QUOTED...................... │
│                              TERMS........................... │
│  REMARKS..................................................... │
│  ............................................................. │
│  RESERVATION REQUESTED BY.................................... │
│  COMPANY...............................PHONE................. │
│  ADDRESS..................................................... │
│  ............................................................. │
│  BILL TO..................................................... │
│  PHONE ☐   VERBALLY ☐   DATE.......................RESERVATION│
│                              TAKEN BY................. │
│  TO BE CONFIRMED BY HOTEL ☐   BY GUEST ☐                     │
│  GTD ☐   PROVISIONAL ☐   GTD BY........................... │
└─────────────────────────────────────────────────────────────┘
```

Figure 3.29 *Room reservation form*

computerized system it is easy to obtain accurate, up-to-date information about the availability of rooms for any date. In the room availability report in Figure 3.30 availability is shown for a five-day period.

Once it has been decided that a hotel is able to supply the guest with the type of room required for the dates specified, the guest is asked to write and confirm the reservation. The guest can either write a letter, or send a fax or email to do this. As soon as the guest sends confirmation of the reservation, the hotel and the guest have entered into a contract. The hotel has agreed to supply the guest with the type of accommodation stated at the price quoted and the guest has agreed to this.

Means of generating additional revenue

Every person working in the front of house area must be able not only to sell bedrooms but also to promote all areas of the hotel. By adopting positive techniques, staff should be able to increase sales by their:

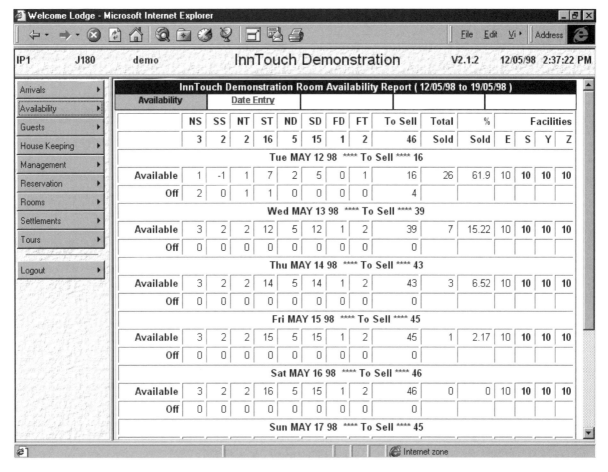

Figure 3.30 *Room availability report*
Courtesy of Innsite Hotel Services Limited

✪ **appearance – they should be neat and tidy and have an air of confidence**

✪ **attitude – they should be cheerful, interested and enthusiastic**

✪ **knowledge – they should have a current knowledge of tariffs and facilities**

✪ **positive questions – they should ask questions such as: Can I get you anything else? Can I reserve a table in the restaurant for you?**

The positive use of body language and communication skills is vital to selling.

Terms of the establishment

Terms refer to the various packages of prices and conditions on offer from the establishment. These can be set in such a way as to attract customers while still making commercial sense to the establishment.

WHITEHALL

THE HOTEL

We have 26 bedrooms - 1 Suite, 6 Superior rooms, 14 Standard Double rooms and 5 Standard Twin rooms, all with en suite, colour television, hairdryer, trouser press, direct dial telephone and newspaper. Luxury bathrobe, iron and ironing board available on request.

	Double Occupancy	Single Occupancy
Penthouse Suite	£220.00	£195.00
Superior Room	£150.00	£95.00
Standard Double	£120.00	£95.00
Standard Twin	£120.00	£95.00
Family Occupancy	*Extra £20.00 per folding bed, sofa bed or cot*	

A special "stand-by" rate is available for bookings made after 12 noon on day of arrival
£80.00 Double or Single Occupancy (first night only)

The above rates include VAT only, they do not include breakfast

Telephone Charges 25p per unit
(Directory Enquiry Calls are charged at 10 units)
Public Telephone also available in Reception

Check out time is 11.00am, to allow staff time to service the rooms the earliest check in time is 2.00pm
We cannot guarantee access prior to this time.

WEEKEND PACKAGES

Package One
£185.00 per couple, per night sharing a double room to include Dinner from the A La Carte menu, accommodation, breakfast for two and VAT.

Package Two
£155.00 per couple, per night sharing a double room to include Dinner from the Chef's Selection menu, accommodation, breakfast for two and VAT.

Please note that a 10% service charge will be added to the total food and bar element of your bill. Although service charge is included in our Weekend Packages, any additional food and bar drinks that you take will be subject to this 10% service charge.
For all conditions of booking see our Wedding and Parties Brochure

WHITEHALL HOTEL, CHURCH END, BROXTED, ESSEX CM6 2BZ · TELEPHONE: (01279) 850603 · FAX: (01279) 850385
HTTP://WWW.WHITEHALLHOTEL.CO.UK

Figure 3.31 *Hotel tariff*
Courtesy of Whitehall Hotel

Title	Includes
European plan	Room only – no meals
Room only	Room only – no meals
Continental plan	Room and breakfast
R and B	Room and breakfast
B and B	Room and breakfast
Dinner, bed and breakfast	Room, dinner and breakfast
Half board	Room, dinner and breakfast
Modified American plan	Room, dinner and breakfast
Demi pension	Room, dinner and breakfast
DBB	Room, dinner and breakfast
Full board	Room, dinner, breakfast, lunch
American plan	Room, dinner, breakfast, lunch
En pension	Room, dinner, breakfast, lunch

Figure 3.32 *Packages offered by hotels*

Tariff

The prices that a hotel charges for its bedrooms are listed in a tariff.
Each hotel sets its own prices for the rooms although in the case of hotels belonging to a company, prices are often set by the company on a national or regional basis. Figure 3.31 is an example of a tariff.

Packages

There are many different packages offered by hotels to guests, some of which are listed in Figure 3.32. Most hotels will allow guests to have lunch instead of dinner. Some hotels include afternoon tea in the package offered for full board, American plan or en pension. The types of packages described above are generally known as terms. At the time of making a reservation, the guest will be asked what terms are required.

Room types

Hotels usually offer guests a variety of different room types. Again, the terminology that each hotel uses varies, but the most common types of rooms are listed in Figure 3.33 on page 118.

Term/symbol	Description
Single	A room for one person
Single with bath	A room for one person with bath
Single with shower	A room for one person with shower
–	A room for one person
Twin	A room with two single beds
Twin with bath	A room with two single beds and bath
Twin with shower	A room with two single beds and shower
=	A room with two single beds
Double	A room with one large bed for two people
Double with bath	A room with one large bed for two people with bath
Double with shower	A room with one large bed for two people with shower
+	A room with one large bed for two people
Executive rooms	Rooms with extra facilities, e.g. trouser press, hairdryer, extra seating area, mini bar
Suite	Bedroom, sitting room and bathroom
Double double	A room with two large beds
Family room	A room capable of taking two adults plus two children (extra beds and cots are usually used)

Figure 3.33 *Types of rooms*

In order that the reservation clerk can sell as many rooms as possible and achieve 100 per cent room occupancy (i.e. sell all the rooms on any one night), it is essential that the reservation clerk knows as much as possible about the hotel. This is called **product knowledge** (see page 98).

It is important to remember that bedrooms are a perishable commodity. This means that there is only one chance to sell a room. If on one night all the bedrooms are not sold, the opportunity to achieve maximum occupancy has been lost. Even if all the rooms are sold the night before and the night after, if they are not all sold on that one night, the opportunity is lost for ever. On the other hand, if the bar does not sell a bottle of champagne tonight, the bar staff still have that bottle of champagne to sell another night – it will not deteriorate or go off and it will be there until it is sold.

From the sale of a room more revenue is generated for the hotel. Guests may use the restaurant, bar, leisure facilities, telephone and other services, which they have to pay for. If the room is not sold, this revenue may be lost.

Rack rates and revenue

Maximum revenue can be achieved by selling the room at the highest published rate. This is generally known as the **rack rate**. It is important to judge how much money will be gained by taking a reservation. If the reservation is for a time when the hotel is likely to be fully booked, there is little point in selling the rooms at a discount. Should the hotel not be full nearer the date the guest wishes to arrive, then it may be possible to consider accepting a reservation where the room rate will be less. It is usual procedure to quote rack rates for a reservation with a long lead-time, i.e. the time between the date the reservation is made and the date of arrival.

Making the best use of rooms

It is important to achieve back-to-back bookings. This means the day one guest leaves a room, another arrives. This provides continuity and also assists in achieving maximum occupancy. Sometimes it is necessary to move guests from one room to another during their stay, particularly if another guest has made a specific request for the room they were occupying, but obviously this is not desirable as it causes the guests upheaval. By poor reservation management, a hotel may have a number of rooms which are available for one night only. It is usually difficult to fill rooms for one night only as most guests stay for at least two nights. Therefore, when recording reservations using a system where rooms are allocated at the initial reservation stage, it is important to pay attention to the rooms allocated to guests in order to avoid a number of one night gaps.

It is also important to ensure that all the expensive rooms are sold, for example all the executive rooms or suites, as more revenue will be earned from these rooms.

Overbooking procedures

Most hotels operate a policy to accept more reservations than they have room for. This is done for two reasons: to cover for any early departures (guests who depart before their scheduled date) and for any no-shows or non-arrivals (guests who make a reservation and do not arrive at the hotel or cancel shortly before they are due to arrive). By accepting more reservations than the hotel can accommodate, the hotel is doing its best to ensure that it will be full every night.

Problems can arise if no guests depart early and if everyone arrives. In this case, the receptionist must find alternative accommodation in a hotel of the same standard nearby and decide which guests will be 'walked', i.e. booked into another hotel. The hotel that originally accepted the reservation must pay for any difference between the room rates charged and also for any taxi fares, etc. incurred by the guest. Excellent communication and social skills are called for when 'walking' a guest!

In most reservation offices, the reservation clerk is set a maximum number of rooms for which overbooking is allowed; if this limit needs to be exceeded, a superior must be contacted for approval.

Referrals

Referrals are made as a last resort. If the hotel is unable to offer the guest the accommodation required for the dates the guest is willing to accept, the reservation clerk should refer the guest to another hotel. In the case of a company hotel, the guest would be referred to the nearest hotel within the company. If the hotel is privately owned and not part of a consortium, the guest would be referred to a hotel with which the reservation clerk is familiar. Hopefully by doing this, the hotel to which the guest is referred will, in turn, refer guests to the first hotel when the occasion arises.

Selling up

Selling up (or up-selling) is a phrase often used in hotels. If a guest requests a room, the reservation clerk must always offer the best room (and usually the most expensive) that the guest is likely to reserve. The reservation clerk should ask the guest the purpose of the intended visit and from this information it can be ascertained what type of room the guest will reserve. For example, if the guest states that it is for a honeymoon, the reservation clerk could suggest that the guest reserves a suite, which will afford more privacy. With experience, it is possible to gauge how much a particular guest would be willing to pay for a room and to sell the guest the particular room type accordingly.

Reservation systems

Depending on the size of the hotel, the type of system used to record reservations varies. Those most commonly used are:

- **bedroom book**
- **conventional chart**
- **density chart**
- **rack system**
- **computer**

Figure 3.34 *Bedroom book*

Bedroom book

The bedroom book (see Figure 3.34) is usually a hard-backed bound book with a page for each day. Down the length of the page the room numbers are written and against the room number is the name of the guest who will be occupying that particular room. For each night of the guest's stay, the name of the guest is written against the room number. For example, for a guest staying for ten nights, the name would be written alongside the room number for ten days.

This system is used only in small hotels since it is labour intensive and it is not easy to see at a glance the total number of rooms available for letting on any particular day.

Conventional chart

A conventional chart is a manual method of recording advance reservations. Usually a page is used for each floor of the hotel and covers one month. The page is divided to show the date at the top of the page and the room numbers and types of rooms down the page (see Figure 3.35, page 122). When a reservation is accepted, the name of the guest is entered in the space according to which room will be occupied and arrows indicate the length of stay. Each square represents one night's stay. It is easy to see at a glance who is occupying which room and when, and it is possible to determine each guest's length of stay very easily.

Density chart

A density chart is another manual method of recording reservations (see Figure 3.36, page 123). A grid is used showing the date and the type and quantities of rooms. A density chart does not show which particular room is being occupied at any one time and does not show the length of stay by an individual guest.

Month _NOVEMBER 2000_

Date / Room	Room Type	1	2	3	4	5	6	7	8	9	10	11	12	13	14	15	16	17	18	19	20	21	22	23	24	25	26	27	28	29	30	31
101	SB								←SMITH→																							
102	TB								←BLACK→					←JONES→						←PETERS→												
103	TB																															
104	SB	←TAYLOR→																														
105	DB									←GREGG→						←SHEPHARD→																
106	DB	←DAVIES→																														
107	SB													←ASLETT→																		
108	SB					←PARSONS→																										
109	TB																															
110	TB																															
111	TB																															
112	DB																															
113	DB																															

Figure 3.35 _Conventional booking chart_

Using a density chart, it is possible to take account of overbooking – usually space is made available at the bottom of each sheet for recording over-bookings.

Rack system

A rack system can be used to provide room status and advance reservation information. Each system can be used independently.

A Whitney rack system is a particular example of a rack system. Reservation details are entered onto a rack slip or shannon (see Figure 3.37) which is filed under the date of arrival in a metal rack. The slips are filed alphabetically in an individual metal carrier, thereby making it easier to see if a guest has a reservation on a particular day.

		1	2	3	4	5	6	7	8	9	10	11	12	13	14	15	16	17	18	19	20	21	22	23	24	25	26	27	28	29	30	31
SB	10	/	/	/	/	/	/	/	/	/	/	/	/	/	/	/	/	/	/	/	/		/	/	/	/	/	/	/	/	/	/
	9	/	/	/	/	/	/	/	/	/	/	/	/	/	/	/	/	/	/	/			/	/	/	/	/	/	/	/	/	/
	8	/		/	/	/		/			/	/	/	/		/	/	/		/	/		/	/			/	/	/		/	/
	7	/		/	/			/			/	/	/	/			/	/					/					/	/		/	
	6		/				/					/	/	/															/			
	5		/									/	/																			
	4											/	/																			
	3											/	/																			
	2																															
	1																															
TB	10	/	/	/	/	/	/	/	/	/	/	/	/	/	/	/	/	/	/	/	/	/	/	/	/	/	/	/	/	/	/	/
	9	/	/	/	/	/	/	/	/	/	/	/	/	/	/	/	/	/	/	/	/		/	/	/	/	/	/	/	/	/	/
	8	/	/	/	/	/	/	/	/	/	/	/	/	/	/	/	/	/	/				/	/	/	/	/	/	/	/	/	/
	7	/	/	/	/	/	/	/	/	/	/	/	/	/	/		/	/					/		/	/	/	/	/			
	6	/	/	/			/		/	/	/	/	/	/	/	/		/	/				/		/		/	/		/		
	5		/			/		/		/	/	/	/	/														/				
	4								/				/	/																		
	3												/	/																		
	2																															
	1																															
DB	5	/	/	/	/	/	/	/		/	/	/	/	/	/	/	/	/	/	/	/	/	/	/	/		/	/	/	/	/	/
	4	/	/	/	/	/	/	/			/	/	/	/	/	/	/	/	/	/	/	/	/		/		/	/	/	/	/	/
	3		/		/								/		/								/		/			/			/	
	2																						/		/						/	
	1																															

Figure 3.36 _Density chart_

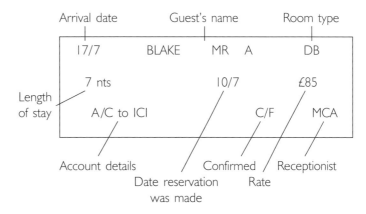

Figure 3.37 _Rack reservation slip_

Computer

Many hotels are now fully computerized and use a specially designed package for recording reservations. A computerized system is very quick and accurate and ensures that the correct details are recorded for each reservation. Using a computer alleviates the need for large amounts of paperwork and provides an efficient service to guests.

However, additional training is required before using the computer and back-up tapes or discs must be taken regularly as a security precaution. Computers have one disadvantage: if the power supply fails, the computer cannot be operated and reservations cannot be accepted or deleted from the system. There are many commercial packages available for use in hotels, for example Innsite, Carahost (used by Forte Hotel) and Fidelio.

Central reservation system

Some hotel companies and consortia also operate a central reservations office to which the guest makes one telephone call. The reservations office makes the reservation on behalf of the guest and has access to all the participating hotels' reservation records, providing a quick efficient service to the guest.

The purpose of a centralized reservations system is to assist people to find hotel accommodation in a particular area with the minimum trouble, and at the same time to help the hotels to fill unlet rooms.

For several years, various large hotel companies and consortia have been operating central bookings offices, enabling people to book accommodation in different hotels operated by that particular group. A centralized reservation system unattached to any hotel or company offers a greater range of hotels over a wider area. How good and how wide the choice is depends upon the number of hotels and hotel groups participating in the scheme. Such a service gives wide coverage to hotels in the United Kingdom and with the inclusion of overseas hotels, the international traveller is able to reserve the accommodation required in areas covered by the service. Likewise it enables hotels within the scheme to widen their catchment area of prospective customers.

To make a booking, the customer telephones the nearest reservation centre and states what is required. These are fed into a computer containing all the relevant information of accommodation available within the scheme and within seconds, the customer is informed of what can be offered. If accepted, the booking is then made with the selected hotel by the reservations service.

For a hotel to join the scheme, it is necessary for the reservations centre to receive certain information about the establishment including the number of different types of rooms to be allocated to the centralized system. The hotel is given a code number for identification and, in some cases, an additional authority code number to prevent false information being given to the reservations service by an outsider.

It is important for the hotel receptionist to keep the reservations service informed of any changes in the availability of the rooms allocated to the service. If, due to the large demand for accommodation, some of the rooms allocated to this service are required by the hotel to cover its own reservations, then these rooms can be withdrawn by the hotel receptionist (usually a supervisor) informing the reservations centre. Unless the reservations service is kept aware of the changes in room availability, double bookings will occur with the attendant problems, complications and loss of goodwill. Conversely, rooms free for letting will not be programmed into the computer and thus will not be offered to prospective customers. Therefore it is essential that the reservation system is kept up to date.

If the hotel has rooms available late at night, it is often possible that the reservation clerk can offer a discount to a private guest requesting a room (known as a chance guest). Each hotel has its own policy relating to discounts.

Reservation service procedure

A person requiring accommodation telephones the nearest reservations service centre and states what is needed – type and price range of room, date of arrival, length of stay and in which area the accommodation is required. The reservations service operator feeds this information into the computer, which produces, in a matter of seconds, a choice of hotels that can satisfy this request. The information appears on a video screen in front of the operator and it is then passed to the enquirer. The reservations service operator answers any further questions by reference to the directory compiled from information given by the hotel when it joined the scheme. When the caller has decided which hotel to stay in, the operator keys this into the computer which automatically deletes that room or rooms from the store of rooms available in that hotel during the required period. The operator now notifies the hotel.

Should the prospective guest cancel the reservation with the hotel itself, the receptionist must inform the reservations service immediately. If this is not done, the reservations service will not know that the room needs to be entered into the computer for reletting. Equally important, if the reservations service is not informed, the hotel will be charged for the reservation. Should the prospective guest cancel with the reservations centre, the centre then takes the necessary action and informs the hotel.

In the case of a no show – the non-arrival of a person who has booked a room and not cancelled – the receptionist should inform the reservations service within 24 hours, otherwise the charge for the reservation could be levied against the hotel.

Cancellations

A reservation of accommodation at a hotel creates a contract between the hotelier and the guest and is enforceable by law. It imposes an obligation on the hotelier to hold a room or rooms at the disposal of the guest for an agreed period of time and on the guest to pay for the accommodation. If either party wishes to alter or cancel the reservation, it must be by mutual agreement or, if they do not agree, subject to liability, they must compensate the other party for any loss sustained.

Cancellation without this consent or failure to arrive on the due date, whatever the reason, entitles the hotelier to compensation, subject to the following set procedure:

1 **The hotelier must take all reasonable steps to relet the accommodation and if successful, must reduce the claim accordingly**

2 **As reletting is possible up to the last day of the booking period, no claim should be made until that period has expired**

3 **Any claims for compensation must exclude such items as food, etc.**

4 **Extra expenses incurred in an attempt to relet (advertising, telephone calls, etc.) can be added to the claim**

5 **If a deposit has been paid, it is not refundable unless the claim is less than the deposit, in which case any balance must be refunded**

In cases which have been decided by courts, hoteliers have received two-thirds of inclusive terms with one-third as value of food.

Illness does not entitle a guest to cancel the contract. A verbal contract may exist, but for court action a written contract is desirable. There must also be an agreement to the booking. An offer by the hotel is not a contract. Also a request for accommodation does not constitute a contract until the hotel has agreed.

In practice, hoteliers tend to follow their own policy on these matters. Usually legal action is only taken by resort hotels where cancellations often result in substantial losses. Some hotels never claim for any cancellations on the grounds that it would be damaging to the goodwill of the hotel. Transient hotels in particular would not be faced with any great loss and the possibility of reletting would be good.

Case study

The Majestic Hotel at Newtown Airport has 750 bedrooms and employs a total of 330 staff. The hotel has a four-star rating and was built in 1998. The relationship between the front office and housekeeping departments has always been very good, largely due to the personalities of the Executive Head Housekeeper and the Head Receptionist.

Because of a large number of staff changes (including promotions within the company), both departments are short staffed and are relying on inexperienced staff.

The Majestic Hotel has a fully networked computer system.

John, one of the new receptionists, takes a reservation from a guest (Mr Stephens) who requires special facilities in his room. Mr Stephens uses a wheelchair. Unfortunately all suitable rooms have already been reserved for the nights Mr Stephens wants to stay but John assures the guest that the housekeeper will ensure that another room will be made available for him. John does not make a note of the guests' requirements.

A few weeks later, Mr Stephens arrives at the hotel. Carrie, the receptionist on duty, notices that Mr Stephens has not been allocated one of the specially adapted rooms and knows that all the adapted rooms are already occupied by other guests. While Mr Stephens is registering, Carrie uses the telephone in the back office to speak to Jane, the duty housekeeper.

Carrie explains the situation to Jane. Jane is working under extreme pressure and tells Carrie that if she had known about Mr Stephens' requirements, she could have made sure that a room was ready for him. Carrie explains that Mr Stephens is at the desk and that she will call Jane back in two minutes.

Carrie returns to the desk and explains to Mr Stephens that his room is not quite ready for him and suggests that he has some coffee in the lounge while he his waiting.

continued

continued

Carrie phones Jane back (who by this time has calmed down a little). Jane agrees to arrange for one of the bedrooms to be adapted for Mr Stephens and Carrie offers to send one of her porters up to help move the furniture. Fortunately all of the equipment (tea making facilities, sockets, etc.) are at a manageable level and the bathroom door is wide enough to accommodate a wheelchair.

Ten minutes later, Jane phones reception and tells Carrie that Mr Stephens' room is now ready for him. Jane then asks Peter the porter to take Mr Stephens and his luggage to his room.

A few minutes later, Mr Stephens phones down to reception to thank Carrie for giving him such a nice bedroom.

Case study discussion questions

1 How could this situation have been avoided?

2 What can be done to improve relationships between the departments?

Front office information systems

Technological advances are being made every day. Some establishments have all the latest equipment with the advantages of improved security and tighter controls, while other establishments prefer to use tried and tested manual systems which the staff are comfortable and familiar with.

There are a number of textbooks concentrating on the development of computerized systems and new technology which will cover this area in more depth. Visits to Hotech and Hospitality exhibitions and reading *Caterer* and *Hotelkeeper* will help you to keep up to date with this constantly developing area.

Computerized systems

Computerized systems are now commonplace in most hotels, which choose to use established systems such as CHAMPS, Innsite or Fidelio. Others use systems developed for a particular hotel company, for example Carahost, as used in Forte Hotels.

A computerized system can eliminate most manual tasks in a reception office. A computer can be used for reservations, billing, pay-roll, ledger accounts, general accounting, conference and banqueting, room status, guest history, room history, sleeper forecasts, daily balancing and messages for guests.

When using a computerized system, it is essential to keep the information 'backed up', i.e. a copy of all the data stored is taken three or more times a day and stored on special disks. This is done as a precaution in case of a system crash or failure, which can be caused by many things, including power surges.

One example of the latest computerized systems available to the industry is InnFront 2000, produced by Innsite. This software package is one of a range of front office solutions which is focused on providing increased revenue to the organization, added control and efficiency in operation and improved service to paying guests. This particular system is aimed at providing a comprehensive front office system for hotels, colleges and other hospitality industries. Management controls can be set up using passwords to control who has access to overbooking and certain parts of the system.

Computer networks

A computer network is a chain of microcomputers that are linked together along with peripherals such as printers. Each user has an intelligent workstation, which is connected to the network, while printers are shared. Some establishments will use a local area network (LAN). Here, microcomputers within the same building are linked together and can share the same data.

Wide areas networks (WAN) link microcomputers across a town, country, continent or worldwide. A WAN creates the possibility of centralized reservation systems and sales and purchase ledger systems. Using such a system, a receptionist at a hotel in Brighton can check availability and make a reservation at a hotel in Perth, using the keyboard in Brighton.

Hilton International has developed their own in-house communications network – Hiltonet; similarly, Holiday Inn uses Holidex.

Automated check-in and check-out

The facility offered by some hotels of automated check-in and check-out is becoming more common, but it will never completely replace the personal role of the hotel receptionist. Automated guest check-in is more popular in the US than in the UK. An automated guest registration system (AGRS) is an electronic device activated by any of the major programmed credit cards.

Customers enter their room requirements via a keyboard system (similar to bank automated cash dispensers). The system will record the customer's credit card details, will register the guest, allocate an appropriate room and dispense a room key. The system will also automatically prepare billing information. This technology provides a solution for offering a 24-hour reception in order to be able to handle late arrivals.

Automated guest check-out systems (AGCS)

AGCS are becoming increasingly popular in the UK but are still used by very few guests. The system allows guests to examine their bills, query charges and settle their accounts by credit card or charge card. In the UK, hotels which use AGCS usually have the system linked into the television screen in bedrooms and guests use the remote control device to access their account information. Some hotels also have terminals at key points, for example in the foyer, in conference rooms or outside the restaurant. The AGCS provides a very speedy check-out for the guest and reduces lengthy queues at busy check-out periods. The system automatically obtains authorization on credit and charge card payments, thus increasing the security for the establishment.

Telecommunications

Developments in telecommunications technology have been rapid since the mid 1990s. Most establishments now have access to the internet and exchange data rapidly using ISDN (Integrated Services Digital Network) lines. ISDN makes possible the flow of voice, data and video between computers in seconds. It works at up to twice the speed of the fastest analogue modem, which saves not only time but money spent on telephone call charges.

Using ISDN it is possible to hold face-to-face meetings with people around the world, as well as discussing and amending the same version of computer-based information in real-time. This will be of great benefit to organizations with outlets in other cities or countries as well as to conference delegates and business people using the outlet.

Outlets use email to communicate more easily, effectively and cheaply with their suppliers and customers. Websites are an excellent way of providing up-to-date information about an organization and are used to promote products and services. Websites can be viewed from anywhere in the world, 24 hours a day, 365 days a year.

Telephone systems

Sophisticated private automatic branch exchange (PABX) switchboards are now more user-friendly and provide many benefits to catering organizations. It is not necessary to employ specialist telephonists, instead the receptionists incorporate the role of switchboard operator into their other roles.

There are three distinct types of PABX:

- ✪ **tailor-made hotel systems**
- ✪ **hotel software and multi-purpose hardware**
- ✪ **multi-purpose software, although the hotel parts are not used by office personnel**

With the advantages and progress of computerization, switchboards now provide a greater range of facilities than merely routing calls. Examples of some facilities available are:

- ✪ **call costing, where every phone calls is logged and automatically charged, thereby avoiding costly disputes over phone charges**
- ✪ **automatic wake-up calls**
- ✪ **baby listening**
- ✪ **personalized service, for example the resident guest's name is revealed on screen when making a call to a hotel department, enabling staff to call the guest by name immediately**

Electronic keys

Electronic keys are plastic cards, the size of a credit card, that have a unique lock combination which is changed with the arrival of each guest. Electronic keys create a secure room without the trouble of replacing lost conventional keys or costly lock changing. The electronic key is placed in a slot-type lock on the room door. When the key is correctly inserted the door will unlock.

Electronic funds transfer at point of sale (EFTPOS)

Credit and debit cards can be processed using EFTPOS. This system allows retailers to debit the credit card company or the bank account of the purchaser. This is done electronically at the point of sale and transfers those funds into the retailer's bank account at the same time or shortly afterwards. The usual checks on the card and signature must be made (see page 107). The advantages of this system are:

- ✪ **greater efficiency – less time is spent with customers making payment**
- ✪ **less cash to handle and therefore fewer security risks**
- ✪ **guaranteed payment once acceptance has been made**

Electronic point-of-sale systems (EPOS)

Driven by the constant need to reduce costs, increase revenue and provide the high level of customer service that today's consumers are increasingly demanding, pubs, bars, restaurants, fast food outlets and cafes all over the UK are introducing new technology systems at a frantic rate, in what has always been a highly competitive sector of the hotel and catering industry market. Many operators have replaced their old-fashioned tills with sophisticated electronic cash registers, preprogrammed with prices for food and drinks. Most large organizations are now giving serious consideration to full-scale EPOS systems, the sort which have long been used in retail outlets to help control stock and cash. EPOS systems are being introduced in ever increasing numbers to many hospitality sector premises. The only way the customer is likely to know that a facility has an EPOS system is when staff use their touch pads or scatter pads, the small touch sensitive panels located behind the bar or counter or sometimes on the cash register itself. The benefits of EPOS are that it improves stock control, gives the management control over cash transactions and frees staff to concentrate on improving customer care rather than having to calculate prices and issue bills.

As well as performing all the normal functions of an electronic cash register, an EPOS system will log all transactions with time, date, items served, cost, method of payment and the member of staff who dealt with the customer. This not only reduces the possibility of fraud by staff but also allows management to introduce incentives for staff who are meeting and exceeding their sales targets. The system will also mean that the busiest times can be better anticipated and will allow better management of staff generally. The detailed management information given by EPOS will mean that stock levels can be monitored more closely, enabling an outlet to hold much smaller levels than would otherwise be the case, thereby improving its cash-flow situation.

Potential benefits of new technology

Figure 3.38 indicates a variety of benefits to customers, staff and the organization of the various types of new technology.

New technology	Benefit to customer	Benefit to staff and organization
Self check-out or check-in	Speedy check-in or check-out – no queuing	Reduces queues and stress – saves staff hours on night duty
Telephone systems	Direct dialling facilities Itemized billing Automatic wake-up calls Message waiting alert	Control over use of phone – can bar extensions Itemized billing reduces lost revenue Automatic wake-up saves staff time
EFTPOS	Reduces fraud – ultimately to reduce costs	Reduces fraud Automatic authorization checks Reduces paperwork
Computer networks	More efficient system – pre-printed registration cards Quicker reservation request response	Increased efficiency Staff can spend more time with customer Increased easy access to data
Electronic room keys	Knowledge of increased security Can keep key on person at all times	Increased security Cheaper then conventional key in long-term

Figure 3.38   *Benefits of new technology*

Legal requirements

Legal requirements affecting other areas of the hotel and catering industry are covered in Units 1, 2 and 5. Here we concentrate on those laws and regulations which affect the day-to-day operation of the front office and housekeeping departments. Figure 3.39 gives a broad outline of some of the rights and responsibilities of the customer and provider.

Legislation	Rights of providers	Rights of customers	Responsibilities of providers	Responsibilities of customers
Tourism (Sleeping Accommodation) Price Display Order 1977		To be aware of price of room before any commitment is made	To ensure a copy of the tariff complying with the order is correctly displayed	
Data Protection Act	To store certain data	To have access to the information held on request	To ensure data is kept confidential To register with the Data Protection Registrar and comply with the Act	
Innkeepers Right of Lien and Innkeepers Act 1878	To seize customers' goods if they are unable to pay a bill, to sell goods by auction after six weeks	To reclaim seized goods after full payment within six weeks of seizure	To advertise the auction one month in advance – to return any surplus after expenses to the guest	To settle all accounts promptly
Hotel Proprietors Act 1956	Non-acceptance of guests who are drunk, verminous, unable or unwilling to pay Limited liability for property not offered for safe keeping	To expect appropriate food, drink and accommodation to be provided Safe keeping of belongings	To ensure food, drink and accommodation are provided as appropriate To provide safe deposit facilities, to minimize thefts from bedrooms and to provide a secure environment	To ensure they are in a fit state to be received To take responsibility for their property
Contract of booking	To expect customers to fulfil their part of contract Can send bill to cover losses	To expect hotel to provide what has been promised Can sue hotel for non-fulfilment	To provide accommodation as promised in the contract	To fulfil their part of the contract

Figure 3.39 *Rights and responsibilities of customers and providers*

The Hotel Proprietors Act 1956

A most important piece of legislation is the Hotel Proprietors Act 1956. This defines a hotel as:

an establishment held out by the proprietor as offering food, drink, and, if required, sleeping accommodation, without special contract, to any traveller presenting himself who appears able and willing to pay a reasonable sum for the services and facilities provided and who is in a fit state to be received.

This legislation covers hotels only since other places which offer accommodation services, such as hospitals, prisons and university residences, do not cater for travellers.

Under this Act, the hotel must ensure the safety of the property of guests. A hotel is liable for the loss of guests' property while they are staying at the hotel, from midnight on the date of arrival to midnight on the day of departure. If loss is caused by the negligence of the hotel or hotel staff, the hotel can be held totally liable, even if it has limited its liability by displaying the statutory notices from the Hotel Proprietors Act 1956 in a prominent place in reception and in guests' bedrooms. If a guest offers property for safe keeping and the receptionist refuses to accept it because, for example, the safe is full or they key is not available at the time, and the property was subsequently stolen, the hotel might be fully liable for the loss. The hotel has no liability if the property is lost or damaged due to negligence by the guest, by an Act of God, or action by the Queen's enemies.

All hotels have safe deposit facilities. Some use a large main safe to which only the reception staff have access. A guest is given a receipt for the property but only broad descriptions are used, for example 'one gold coloured ring' and not 'one gold ring' as you cannot be sure it is gold. Other hotels have individual safe deposit boxes which require two keys to be inserted at the same time to gain access. The guest is issued with one key and the receptionist has the other key.

Trade description: The Tourism (Sleeping Accommodation) Price Display Order 1977

This states that the current minimum and maximum prices charged per night for accommodation must be displayed. If the prices include VAT, this must be stated. If there is a service charge, this must be included in the price. Any meals included in the price must also be stated.

Immigration (Hotel Records) Order 1972

This states that certain information must be provided by guests when they arrive at a hotel at which they will be sleeping. All guests over the age of 16 years must provide the following information:

- **full name**
- **nationality**
- **date of arrival**

Anyone who does not fall into one of the following categories is known as an alien and must provide additional information:

- **British passport holders**
- **citizens of The Republic of Ireland (Eire)**
- **Commonwealth citizens**
- **members of NATO armed forces serving in the United Kingdom**
- **foreign nationals serving with the United Kingdom's armed forces**
- **foreign diplomats, envoys and their staff (this is under the Diplomatic Privileges Act 1964)**
- **citizens of the European Union**

The following additional information is required:

- **passport number and date and place of issue**
- **next destination**
- **signature**

Guests do not have to complete the registration form or book themselves; it can be done by a third party. The hotel must keep the registration documents for 12 months. They may be inspected by the police or representatives of the Secretary of State for the Home Office.

Disability Discrimination Act

The provisions of the Disability Discrimination Act will be in force by the end of 2002.

The Disability Discrimination Act brings in new laws and measures aimed at ending the discrimination which many disabled people face. The Act will affect anyone who provides goods, services or facilities to members of the public whether paid for or free. It will be against the law to

✪ **refuse to serve someone who is disabled, for example a hotel owner will not be able to refuse to let a room to a disabled person**

✪ **offer a disabled person a service which is not as good as the service being offered to other people, for example a restaurant manager will not be able to insist that a person with a facial disfigurement sits out of sight of other customers**

✪ **provide a service to a disabled person on terms which are different from the terms given to other people, for example it will not be possible to ask a disabled person for a bigger deposit when they are booking a holiday**

In some situations there will be exceptions to the law. If the health and safety of the disabled person or other people would be in danger, it would not be against the law to refuse to provide the service to a disabled person or to provide it on different terms. Other exceptions would arise if the customer was not capable of understanding the terms of a contract, or if providing the service or the same standards of service would deny service to other customers.

It will be against the law for someone to run a service or provide goods or facilities in a way which makes it impossible or unreasonably difficult for a disabled person to use the service or goods. For example, a restaurant which does not allow animals will not be able to refuse admission to a disabled person with a guide dog. Organizations will have to remove physical obstructions (for example by widening entrance doors) or provide some other ways of letting disabled people use their services if it is reasonable to do so.

Data Protection Act

The increasing use of computer systems to store data on individuals led to the introduction of the Data Protection Act (DPA) in May 1986. Since then, the Act has been extended to cover all information, whether held on computer or paper-based.

Under this Act, individuals who have data held on them have a range of rights in civil law, including:

✪ **rights of access to the data**

✪ **rights to apply to have any inaccuracies in the data rectified and, in certain circumstances, to have the information erased**

✪ **rights to compensation for inaccuracy of data**

✪ **rights to compensation for loss, destruction or unauthorized disclosure of data**

The DPA requires that all organizations which hold personal data about individuals must register with the Data Protection Registrar and comply with the Data Protection Act. The Act seeks to regulate the way in which data are gathered, stored and disclosed to third parties.

The Act establishes eight data protection principles with which data users must comply. Data users are defined as individuals, corporations or other agencies which control the processing of data. The eight principles, which in reality are a set of points of good practice to which data users should aspire, are as follows:

1 The information held shall be obtained and processed **fairly** and **lawfully**. Data would be said to have been obtained unfairly if the provider was deceived or misled about the purpose for which the information was being obtained.

2 Personal data shall be held only for one or more **specified** and **lawful** purposes. A contravention of this particular principle would be, for example, when an organization holds personal information for staff training purposes but chooses to use it for the selection of staff for redundancy.

3 Data shall not be disclosed to persons other than those named in the registration document, nor for any other purpose than that registered under the Act.

4 Personal data held for any purpose or purposes shall be **adequate**, **relevant** and **not excessive** in relation to the registered purpose. An organization which holds data which are unrelated to the purpose for which it is registered or is clearly holding far more than are needed to satisfy the purpose, will be in breach of this principle.

5 Personal data shall be **accurate** and **updated** as and when necessary. If, for example, an organization holds a list of customers who have exceeded their annual credit limit but makes no attempt to update the list when further payments are made, it is likely to be considered as having contravened this principle.

6 Personal information held for any purpose or purposes shall not be kept for longer than is necessary. A hotel which holds a prize draw and which uses a computer to store the names and addresses of those entering, should destroy those data at the end of the promotion.

7 An individual shall be entitled, at reasonable intervals and without undue delay or expense, to know whether information is held on him or her and to have **access** to any data which do exist; also to have any data **corrected** or **erased** as appropriate.

8   The data user shall take reasonable security measures to guard against unauthorized access to, alteration, disclosure, accidental loss or destruction of the personal data.

The extent to which personal data is stored throughout the hospitality and catering industry means that the Act has important implications for the industry. Databases for marketing and promotional work, in hotel leisure clubs, guests' accounts in hotels, to name but a few, involve the collection and storage of personal data on individuals. Managers therefore need to be aware of the principles of the Data Protection Act and the extent to which it affects their own particular organization.

Visit www.dataprotection.gov.uk for more information about the Data Protection Act.

Trading Law

The laws governing trading in general are lengthy and complex. Here we give brief information about the relevant legislation but you should consult texts specializing in this area for more detailed information or look in Croner's *Catering* (available in both paper and CD ROM formats).

Trading law is divided into civil law (The Misrepresentation Act 1967) and criminal law (The Trades Descriptions Act 1968). There are also laws governing health and safety, food safety and weights and measures (see pages 185 and 186–92).

A breach of the criminal law will lead to a prosecution of the offender, which could be an individual manager as well as the company, by a Trading Standards Officer. Most cases go to the Magistrates Court. If guilty, a fine can be imposed and, if the case goes to the Crown Court, a jail sentence could be imposed.

A breach of the civil law, on the other hand, concerns disputes between individuals or companies. You could be sued by the other party for compensation, normally in the County Court.

The Misrepresentation Act 1967

There are three main types of possible misrepresentation:

○ **innocent misrepresentation**: This is where the person who spoke or wrote the misrepresentation really did believe it was true and had good grounds for believing it to be true, for example, a receptionist could repeat in good faith some inaccurate information printed in a brochure.

- ✪ **negligent misrepresentation**: This is where the person who wrote or spoke the misrepresentation really did believe it was true but had no good grounds for so believing.
- ✪ **fraudulent misrepresentation**: This is the most serious type – it occurs either when a person simply tells lies or says any statement without caring one way or another about its truth.

Most cases which come to court involve negligent misrepresentation. Managers and others making statements about their goods or services must be very careful to ensure that they are telling the truth, not just relying on what they think is the truth.

The Trades Descriptions Act 1968

It is illegal to make a false statement about services, accommodation or facilities, for example, a brochure could falsely claim that the restaurant was air-conditioned.

Fidelity bond

Cashiers handle a large sum of money every day and are also responsible for a large change float held in a safe. Honesty is one of the prime qualifications for a person handling money. Most cashiers will be 'bonded' with an insurance company so that the hotel is covered against a dishonest act by one of the cashiers.

Revision questions

1 Which one of the following information sheets should the housekeeper consult when preparing the duty rota?

   (a) In-house list
   (b) Housekeeper's report
   (c) Occupancy forecast
   (d) Budget   (1 mark)

2 Non-verbal communication involves:

   (a) Departmental memos and printouts
   (b) Facial gestures and eye contact
   (c) Telephone conversations   (1 mark)

3 The practice of repairing things before they get worse is known as:

   (a) Routine maintenance
   (b) Daily service
   (c) Preventative maintenance
   (d) Special service   (1 mark)

4 The housekeeper needs to discuss room occupancy with the:

   (a) Hall porter
   (b) Receptionist
   (c) Handy man
   (d) Chef   (1 mark)

5 What are acid cleaners used for?   (2 marks)

6 What are solvent based cleaners used for?   (2 marks)

7 What type of lighting is most suitable in a reception area?   (1 mark)

8 What are the main points of the Fire Precautions Act 1971?   (5 marks)

9 Name six pieces of electrical cleaning equipment that can be used in the accommodation services area.   (6 marks)

10 Name ten pieces of manual cleaning equipment that can be used in the accommodation services area.   (10 marks)

11 When a guest asks for a room to be reserved from the 27th–29th inclusive, when will the guest arrive and when will the guest leave?   (2 marks)

12 Why is overbooking done in some hotels?   (2 marks)

13 How long must guest registration details be kept after arrival?   (1 mark)

14 Front office staff can use a document to show which guests are expected to arrive on a particular day. What is this called?   (1 mark)

Keys to attainment

These are key skills or aspects of key skills that are central to the Accommodation and Front Office unit. The key to attainment shows that the relevant aspect of the key skill has also been achieved. You will of course need to develop and practise the key skill during your lessons and in your private studies.

Communication, level 3

When you are:	You should have achieved the following key skills evidence:
Researching and collecting information on facilities, products and services provided by accommodation and front office operations	C3.2 Read and synthesize information from two extended documents about a complex subject. One of these documents should include at least one image.
Presenting a summary of the impact of environmental and technological changes	C3.1b Make a presentation about a complex subject, using at least one image to illustrate complex points.
Producing the results of your investigations into accommodation and front office services	C3.3 Write two different types of documents about complex subjects. One piece of writing should be an extended document and include at least one image.

Signposts

These are naturally occurring opportunities for the development of key skills through your learning and assessment. You will not necessarily achieve the signposted key skill through your evidence for the Accommodation and Front Office unit. You will need to develop additional evidence elsewhere to ensure that you meet the requirements of the key skills units fully.

Communication, level 3

When you are:	There may be opportunities for you to develop the following key skills evidence:
Researching facilities, products and services provided by accommodation and front office operations	C3.1a Contribute to a group discussion about a complex subject.

Information Technology, level 3

When you are:	There may be opportunities for you to develop the following key skills evidence:
Researching facilities, products and services provided by accommodation and front office operations using IT	IT 3.1 Plan and use different sources to search for and select information required for two different purposes.
Presenting a summary of the impact of environmental and technological changes	IT 3.2 Explore, develop and exchange information and derive new information to meet two different purposes.
Producing the results of your investigations into accommodation and front office services	IT 3.3 Present information from different sources for two different purposes and audiences. Include at least one example of text, one example of images and one example of numbers.

Improving own learning and performance, level 3

When you are:	There may be opportunities for you to develop the following key skills evidence:
Working on your investigation into accommodation and front office operations	LP 3.1, 3.2 and 3.3

Customer service

This unit will provide you with a good understanding of customer service provision in hospitality and catering outlets. You will focus on learning about customer service and the procedures and practices used by supervisors in outlets to maintain and improve the standards of quality customer service. All customers have different needs and will expect their needs to be met with courtesy and efficiency.

In this unit you will learn:

- **why excellent customer service is so important in hospitality and catering**

- **how to adapt customer service techniques to meet the needs and wants of different types of customers and situations**

- **about quality customer service standards**

- **how to plan, measure, monitor and evaluate customer service procedures and practices**

The knowledge and skills you learn in this unit will be useful when studying other units – it will also help you when working in outlets, whether on work experience, work shadowing or in a part-time job.

Hospitality and catering organizations sometimes lose sight of the fact that without customers there would be no business. Their policies and actions do not always take account of the fact that customers are the most important people to their organization. Rather than being an interruption to the work of any hospitality and catering organization, customers are the very purpose of its existence. It is only when organizations begin to put the customer at the centre of all activity that a true customer service approach has begun.

Customers in hospitality and catering take many different forms. They may be enjoying their leisure time with a relaxed meal out of the home, or they may be business clients attending a conference. They will come from right across the age range, from different ethnic and cultural backgrounds, different social classes and varying home circumstances.

Providing excellent customer service

Presentation

First impressions count in any business but particularly in hospitality and catering where dealing with customers is such an important part of the work. Customers can be classified as internal, such as a member of another department within the outlet or organization, or external, such as a member of the public or from a different organization. Figure 4.1 lists some types of internal and external customers likely to be found in a hospitality and catering organization.

It is often said that 'you only get one chance to make a first impression' – and that is very true in hospitality and catering organizations. Most customers will use their first impressions of an outlet to determine whether they will actually venture inside, or whether they will place an order for food at the bar, having caught a glimpse of the chef.

The external appearance of an outlet will create an impression. If the paintwork is flaking and if the plants in the tubs and baskets are dead, customers may think that the exterior is not looked after and that the kitchens and other areas not normally seen by the public must be much worse.

Outlets which are part of a larger group may have to conform to standards of external presentation – for example they may have to display certain signs, fly the corporate flag, etc.

Other first impressions are created by the staff.

Internal customers	External customers
Other staff members in same department	Customers
Other staff members in other departments	Guests
All supervisors and managers	Patients
All members of staff in a head office	Suppliers
All members of staff in other outlets owned by the same organization	Trade organizations
	Environmental Health Officers
	Police
	Fire Authority
	AA/RAC inspectors
	ETB inspectors

Figure 4.1 *Internal and external customers of a catering or hospitality organization*

Figure 4.2 *The Grand Hotel, Brighton*
Courtesy of The Grand Hotel, Brighton

Personal presentation

How the staff are dressed will create an impression. If uniforms are provided these should be worn correctly. All clothing must of course be clean and well pressed.

Organizations usually have standards which staff must meet in terms of their personal presentation. An example of such a standard (adapted from one used at The Grand Hotel in Brighton) is shown in Figure 4.3.

Shoes should be clean and well heeled and of a suitable type for the activities being undertaken; for example, it would be very unlikely that a receptionist in a five-star hotel would be wearing trainers.

In general, jewellery should be kept to a minimum. In certain areas of the industry, staff are not normally allowed to wear any jewellery for hygiene and safety reasons.

Make-up should be worn discreetly. Again, staff working in some areas will not be permitted to wear make-up.

Hair should generally be worn in a style which is suitable to the member of staff's job role and to the establishment. Hair should of course always be clean.

Personal hygiene is extremely important. Many members of staff will be working in very close proximity to customers and body odours will be offensive.

Standard: Appearance and personal hygiene Staff name: Check completed by:			Date:	
	Always adhered to	**Sometimes adhered to**	**Never adhered to**	**Comments**
Name badges worn in correct position				
Correct uniform worn				
Jewellery				
Make-up				
Hair				
Personal hygiene				

Figure 4.3 *Standard form for personal presentation*

Posture is also important – not only does a member of staff who is slouched in a chair or leaning on one elbow look inattentive, it is also very bad for the general posture of the member of staff. In the hospitality and catering industry most jobs involve lengthy periods of standing. Good posture is essential in order to avoid potential back problems.

Communication skills

Effective communication skills are essential in the hospitality and catering industry. Good communication is a key aspect of good customer service in all activities in the industry.

Speaking on the phone

When using the telephone you should always be prepared. The following guide should be used when using the telephone at work.

When making a call:

✪ **greet the person answering the call and identify yourself**
✪ **ask for the person required**
✪ **confirm who you are speaking to**

- ✪ outline your reason for calling
- ✪ listen for the reply
- ✪ ask questions to clarify the response
- ✪ make notes
- ✪ clarify by repeating the main points
- ✪ thank the person and confirm any further action you are going to take
- ✪ follow up action resulting from the call as soon as possible

When answering the telephone:

- ✪ answer promptly
- ✪ greet the caller and identify your establishment, the department and yourself
- ✪ offer help
- ✪ listen to the caller
- ✪ make notes
- ✪ ask questions to clarify
- ✪ offer the appropriate service (book a table/room/conference)
- ✪ provide information
- ✪ confirm details by repeating the main points
- ✪ give the caller the opportunity to ask more questions
- ✪ thank the caller and say goodbye
- ✪ carry out what you need to do immediately

Communicating face to face

When dealing with customers face to face, the following guidelines should be followed:

- ✪ Remember that first impressions count
- ✪ Be smart and clean
- ✪ Have good personal hygiene
- ✪ Check your posture
- ✪ Take a pride in yourself and you will gain respect from others
- ✪ Be yourself, but be professional
- ✪ Use your personality
- ✪ Use your body language to show interest and be welcoming
- ✪ Recognize body language in others and react to it – it gives clues as to the reaction of others, their mood and state of mind

- Develop active listening – give full attention, show interest, identify the main items and then respond and take action
- Respond positively – clarify and confirm requests
- Gather more information using open questions
- Provide solutions
- Consider how you speak, noting volume, tone, pitch and pace
- Make eye contact to ensure positive communication
- Use the name of the person to show recognition and friendliness
- Smile

Communicating in writing

Writing letters is an important part of many types of activity in hospitality and catering. Below are some key pointers to good letter writing.

Effective letter writing requires the recognition and observance of three basic principles:

1 the need to define the purpose of the letter
2 the need always to consider the reader of the letter
3 the need always to use language appropriate to these two requirements

The following points are important to all forms of written communication:

- Be clear – this means avoiding ambiguity, making the correct use of punctuation and placing adjectives and adverbs in the right context.
- Be concise – brevity is accomplished by the elimination of 'padding' caused most often through needless clichés and meaningless phrases.
- Be correct – not only are facts, figures, data, detail, information, etc. important, but, when writing, so is construction, i.e. grammar, punctuation and especially spelling.
- Be complete – this means providing all the information and answers to satisfy the reader and the purpose of the letter or other form of written communication.
- Be courteous – choice and use of words create the tone of any written text. The right tone will convey an image to the reader of a warm, helpful, interested human being. Make sure that the recipient's name is spelt correctly.
- Ensure the layout is neat and attractive.
- Avoid the use of jargon, use direct words instead.
- Make sure that all enclosures are included.

Product knowledge

All staff should be aware of the products and services that their organization provides. Staff should also have detailed knowledge of the products and services that are provided by their department or area of the organization.

Some staff, particularly those new to their job, will take time to settle into their role and gain the knowledge and experience necessary to carry it out to the full. Induction training followed by detailed training on the services, products and systems of the organization should give these staff the confidence to sustain a high level of customer service and feel a valued member of the team. Good information and awareness can help staff to:

✪ **inform customers of prices and features of the products and services on offer**

✪ **suggest alternatives if the customer's first choice is not available**

✪ **give detailed information of particular services – in hospitality and catering it is often 'the little things' that either make or break the total experience for the customer**

✪ **raise the general level of awareness of other services and facilities that the organization can offer**

Understanding quality customer service standards

What customer service standards are

A key ingredient of providing excellent customer service is the need for standards. There are broadly two types of standards: operational and competence.

Operational standards

Operational standards tend to specify what has to be done or said, for example:

✪ **Receptionists wear name badges and are encouraged to smile and make eye contact with guests as they approach the desk and use their names whenever possible**

✪ **Telephones should be answered before the third ring, with a greeting followed by the name of the hotel or the internal department**

Competence standards

Competence standards are designed to describe the action an individual needs to follow to perform a task competently; they specify the 'how'. Competence standards usually describe the actions as detailed performance criteria and many hospitality and catering organizations base their competence standards on the National Performance Standards (found for each job role in the National Vocational Qualification (NVQ) Framework). For example, to present a positive personal image to customers, you should:

✪ **always treat customers in a courteous and helpful manner, especially when your own circumstances are under stress**

✪ **consistently maintain standards for appearance and behaviour**

✪ **ensure equipment and supplies used in transactions with customers are available, up to date and in good order**

✪ **actively seek opportunities for improving working relationships with customers**

✪ **ensure own behaviour consistently conveys a positive image of the organization to current and potential customers**

If these criteria are met, members of staff will have followed a process that ensures they have performed competently. By regularly measuring and assessing both operational and competence standards, it is possible to judge when and how excellent customer service is being provided.

Setting standards of care

Some examples of customer care standards are shown in Figure 4.4.

Activity	Minimum standard to be achieved	When/how checked
Answering the telephone	Answer before the third ring	Use of mystery guest on a regular basis
Greeting at reception	Acknowledged within 20 seconds	Front office manager to check
Ensuring toilets are clean	Checked and cleaned every hour with signed declaration clearly visible	Head housekeeper to check
Ensuring staff have skills and product knowledge	Full awareness of operational standards	Use of a mystery guest

Figure 4.4 *Customer care standards*

Case study

The Weary Traveller, a motorway service station, has accepted a booking for a coach party en route to Bournemouth for a holiday. The 37 passengers require coffee and biscuits – the driver and courier require tea. The party is on a tight schedule and will only stay for 45 minutes in order to reach Bournemouth in time for an evening show.

Five days before the party is due to arrive, Mrs Blake, the organizer, phones to change the order to 35 coffees, two

continued

continued

fruit juices and two teas. She also mentions that there will be four passengers who are wheelchair users.

On the day, the coach is delayed on the motorway by severe weather and the party arrives one hour late.

The courier discovers that there is no access for those using wheelchairs and that the fruit juices are not available. Several members of the coach party complain about the state of the toilets and the lack of seating (this is because another large party booked for the same day has arrived on time). Several passengers do not receive a drink because of the lack of time. The party leaves very unhappy.

The next day, Mrs Blake writes a long letter of complaint and refuses to pay the bill until a satisfactory explanation has been given.

Case study discussion questions

1 What has happened?

2 If you were working at The Weary Traveller, how would you reply to Mrs Blake?

3 Set some operational standards for large parties.

Implementing a customer care programme

When a hospitality and catering organization is implementing a customer care programme, there is always the danger that the staff will think their work is over when a programme is finally put in place. In reality, this is far from the case and is likely to be when the hard work really begins. If the staff and management see the customer care programme as just another campaign, it will start to falter from day one, and a further campaign will need to be launched at a later date.

All those involved with the programme must realize that it is not a 'one off' but is part of the process of creating a different culture within the organization – one which has customers as its focus. A customer care programme is not a 'quick fix' which will sweep away all the organization's problems overnight. Rather it is a process which will take time to achieve its objective of excellence in customer service.

Customers' needs and expectations are constantly changing in the hospitality and catering business, so that any customer care programme must be flexible enough to meet the requirements of an increasingly discerning public.

All of these factors point to the need for constant monitoring and evaluation of the customer care programme to ensure that it is meeting the aims set by the organization. Monitoring and evaluation is the last link in the chain of customer care which begins with setting objectives and investigating customer needs, and moves through training of staff and managers to looking at alterations to existing systems. Monitoring is concerned with looking at how the customer care programme is operating in the organization, while evaluation means measuring its effectiveness. From a management perspective, evaluation is very important, because, 'if you can't measure it, you can't manage it'.

The need for monitoring and evaluation

Those hospitality and catering professionals who take quality seriously, enthuse and stimulate those working with them. To them, customer care can become a way of life, even a crusade. Following the route to excellence in customer service may change not only the way they operate at work, but also their whole attitude to life in general, with a greater degree of openness and fairness. Sadly, not all staff within a hospitality and catering organization may share this same zeal or be given the opportunity to see a customer care programme through to its completion. Pressures on senior management may force them to transfer their time and commitment away from the customer care programme to some other function. At the same time, some staff may become sceptical about the benefits of the programme or there may be breakdowns in communication within the organization.

These sorts of problems highlight the need for effective monitoring and evaluation of any customer care programme. Measuring effectiveness allows an organization to do a number of things. It can:

✪ **develop training**

✪ **increase customer service awareness**

✪ **focus efforts**

✪ **evaluate the programme according to pre-determined criteria**

- ✪ identify strengths and weaknesses
- ✪ reward staff accordingly
- ✪ monitor progression
- ✪ quantify achievements

In practice, most organizations use monitoring and evaluation to achieve a mixture of the above points.

The type of questions which should be asked of any customer care programme include the following:

- ✪ **What are the successes of the customer care programme?**
- ✪ **Are the original objectives of the programme still valid?**
- ✪ **How does the performance to date measure against the established criteria?**
- ✪ **What are the major priorities for action to put things right?**
- ✪ **How can the organization build on these successes?**
- ✪ **What are the weaknesses of the programme?**
- ✪ **Have the customers' expectations of service quality changed?**
- ✪ **In which areas do improvements need to be made?**

Programme evaluation in practice

There are three main elements to the evaluation of any customer care programme:

1 **setting performance standards/criteria**
2 **measuring to see if the standards are being met**
3 **implementing measures to rectify any shortcomings**

Setting performance standards

When hospitality and catering organizations strive for excellence in customer care, it soon becomes clear that it is not enough simply to encourage staff to 'give the customers a better standard of customer care'. There comes a point when the management has to define just what 'better' means. Employees need to know the standards against which their performance will be measured. Staff will need both a clear job description and a set of performance standards or performance criteria for each of the tasks they are responsible for.

Staff role   Customer Service Assistant

Task   Serving a light meal or snack to a customer

Step one   Greeting the customer

Standards   a)   Smile pleasantly while you wish the customer a pleasant good morning/afternoon/evening
b)   Offer the customer a menu if he or she doesn't have one
c)   Use the customer's name if you know it

Step two   Taking the customer's order

Standards   a)   Be familiar with all items on the menu
b)   Ask the customer for his/her order
c)   Answer any questions the customer may have precisely and courteously
d)   If something is requested which is not on the menu, suggest an alternative
e)   Accept any special orders graciously
f)   Thank the customer for the order and let him or her know how long the meal will take to prepare

---

Figure 4.5   *Typical performance standards in customer care*

The difference between operational and competence standards is discussed on pages 153–4.

Devising and implementing performance standards is a very time-consuming task and one which, if done properly, will call for an investment of financial resources from the organization.

Large hospitality and catering organizations, with extensive personnel and training departments, may well carry out the task themselves. Smaller organizations are likely to appoint a consultant to devise the standards on their behalf or use criteria already available through professional bodies and other industry organizations.

Figure 4.5 shows an example of typical performance standards which could be used in a restaurant, hotel or any catering outlet. This is only a small section of a typical set of performance standards, but it shows the detail which is needed if the exercise is to be a success.

In addition to the detailed performance standards for specific job tasks, there will be the overall objectives of the customer care programme itself, which again must be specific and detailed. Examples of objectives of customer care programmes in hospitality and catering could be:

- ✪ **for a restaurant to achieve a 15 per cent reduction in the number of complaints**
- ✪ **for a hotel to achieve a 10 per cent increase in bookings sold**
- ✪ **to achieve a 10 per cent increase in the 'excellent' category for responses to a customer satisfaction survey**
- ✪ **for a hotel a achieve a 15 per cent increase in bednights sold to business customers**

Using the objectives of the customer care programme and specific performance indicators as the yardstick against which the effectiveness of the programme can be measured, the organization is now in a position to consider the most appropriate ways in which the measurement can take place.

Measuring to see if the standards are being met

Whereas a company in the manufacturing sector of the economy can reasonably easily set standards for the quality of its products and measure to see if the standards are being met, this process is much more difficult in a service sector industry such as hospitality and catering. However, although a difficult task, it is essential that any organization which is committed to improving customer care develops systems and procedures to measure the effectiveness of its activities. Some of the main techniques for measuring to see if standards are being met are:

- ✪ **surveys**
- ✪ **observation**
- ✪ **recording informal feedback**
- ✪ **checking financial data**
- ✪ **analysing customer data**

Surveys

Surveys are the most common method of monitoring levels of performance in customer care. An organization will use a survey as part of a customer care programme to see if the targets it set itself are being achieved in reality. A survey provides a 'snapshot' of an organization's health at a particular point in time. If designed and carried out effectively, surveys are important to management since they measure the satisfaction levels within the organization and provide crucial information on which decisions can be made.

Surveys as part of a customer care programme can be directed at:

- ✪ **customers**
- ✪ **staff**
- ✪ **internal customers**
- ✪ **management**
- ✪ **non-users**

Customers

A customer satisfaction survey at a restaurant or a survey of visitors at a hotel pub or club will provide valuable information about how customers perceive their experience, how they feel about the standard of service and the attitude of the staff, and how any queries have been dealt with, etc. Customer comment forms and suggestion boxes may play a part here. An example of a customer care feedback form is shown in Figure 4.6.

Staff

It is important to seek and act continually on the views of staff at the 'sharp end' of customer care. Without their continuing support, the programme will not succeed. An employee attitude survey will give them the chance to have their ideas and concerns formally noted. Management will be able to see if particular concerns are being expressed by more than one individual and act accordingly.

Please rate and comment on the following areas:

Service:

☐ Excellent ☐ Good ☐ Fair ☐ Poor

Comments:

_____
_____
_____
_____
_____
_____

Attitude:

☐ Excellent ☐ Good ☐ Fair ☐ Poor

Comments:

_____
_____
_____
_____
_____
_____

Facility:

☐ Excellent ☐ Good ☐ Fair ☐ Poor

Comments:

_____
_____
_____
_____
_____
_____

If you contacted our staff with requests during your stay, did we respond to your satisfaction?

☐ Yes ☐ No

Comments:

_____
_____
_____
_____
_____

If utilised, please rate the following:

	Excellent	Good	Fair	Poor
Porters	☐	☐	☐	☐
Front Desk	☐	☐	☐	☐
Bar	☐	☐	☐	☐
Restaurants	☐	☐	☐	☐
Room Service	☐	☐	☐	☐
Leisure Club	☐	☐	☐	☐

Are there any other services that you would like us to offer?

_____
_____
_____

Thank you for taking the time to comment.

Richard Baker
General Manager

Assuming that you will need hotel accommodation in the future, would you choose to stay at another De Vere Hotel?

☐ Yes ☐ No

During your stay, did you encounter an employee who provided exceptional De Vere service?

_____
_____
_____
_____
_____
_____

What was the primary purpose of your visit?

☐ Business
☐ Conference/Group Meeting
☐ Pleasure

Name _____
Company _____
Address _____
_____
_____
Post code _____
Phone _____
Dates of stay _____

The Grand, Brighton, King's Road, Brighton, East Sussex BN1 2FW.

Figure 4.6 *Customer care feedback form*
Courtesy of The Grand Hotel, Brighton

Internal customers

We have seen that all staff in an organization have 'customers', whether or not they deal with the public face to face. Internal customers are colleagues in the same organization who may be in a different department but whose co-operation and support is vital.

Management

The managers in the organization should be surveyed routinely to see if they are clear about their role to achieve total customer satisfaction. If the management are unclear or unhappy about the culture of the organization, these fears may be transmitted to other staff and even customers.

Non-users

It may be useful to find out why people are not using a particular facility or location but are choosing to spend their money on competitor products and services instead. Such a survey, which is normally carried out in the street or door-to-door, may highlight aspects of poor customer service which could be put right.

Observation

Observing what people do and say, whether they are customers, managers or staff, can provide useful feedback on the effectiveness of any customer care programme. It is common for an employee, who has been given clear performance standards to achieve, to be observed in the workplace by the line manager. Indeed, part of the evaluation process of the programme may be a manager observing staff and recording their progress over a period of time. Staff in certain hospitality and catering organizations may also be tested from time to time by management on matters such as pricing and product knowledge.

Customers may be observed in order to gain a fuller picture of their satisfaction levels. Staff may be given the task of 'mingling' with customers to listen to their views; people are often more open with their comments if they think their answers or comments are not going to be recorded on a questionnaire. The sectors of the industry where observation of customers is a particulary useful technique include restaurants and cafes, pubs, clubs, etc.

Recording informal feedback

Any hospitality and catering organization which is striving to improve its customer care will go out of its way to seek customers views in a variety of ways. To give the whole programme credibility in the eyes of customers, it is vital that their views are listened to and acted upon. There are many occasions in the course of a normal day when staff in hospitality and catering outlets will have the opportunity to receive informal comments from guests, clients and visitors. It is important for staff to have the chance to pool this feedback since it can be an invaluable management aid. It may be that staff discussion groups could be held once a week when the informal feedback could be discussed and perhaps recorded. Alternatively, customer feedback sheets could be issued to all staff for them to record comments as they receive them, for analysis at a later date.

Checking financial data

Customer care programmes with financial objectives as part of their overall aims, for example for a hotel to achieve a 5 per cent increase in conference business within 12 months, can be evaluated relatively easily. If the organization has a well-structured management information system, a check on sales figures should provide the necessary evidence.

Analyzing customer data

Data on customers, such as the frequency of bookings, satisfaction levels, volume of repeat business, level of customer spend, etc., are available from both surveys and internal records. Analyzing such information, either manually or with the help of a computer-based system, will allow managers to see if performance standards and specific objectives of the customer care programme are being met.

Implementing measures to rectify any shortcomings

If the process of measuring actual performance against the performance standards and criteria shows that targets are not being met, measures to rectify the situation will need to be implemented as soon as possible to maintain the impetus of the customer care programme. The measurement exercise may highlight the need for alterations to existing systems and work patterns in order to improve matters, or perhaps more training for staff or management. Once the measures have been put in place, the process of monitoring and evaluation will continue using a mixture of the techniques described above.

Maintaining the momentum

We have seen that the planning, implementation and evaluation of a customer care programme in hospitality and catering is a very complex, time-consuming and resource intensive process. Any faltering on the part of management or staff could lead to the whole exercise failing to meet its objectives. One of the most important tasks for management is to make sure that the momentum of the programme is maintained throughout. Some managers adopt a campaign approach to this by involving staff in devising slogans, having T-shirts, posters and pens printed with slogans, and arranging extra social and sporting activities within the organization. Such an approach is particularly useful in the early stages of the customer care programme to build staff loyalty to the scheme.

Managers and staff should not be afraid of publicizing achievements within the programme; perhaps a performance standard has not only been met but exceeded. Newsletters and notice boards should be used to communicate such examples to all staff to help maintain the momentum. Above all, it is essential that managers appreciate what their staff are doing to achieve excellence in customer care and reward them accordingly.

Good and bad customer service

Defining what is good and bad service is not always an easy matter. One person's idea of good service in a restaurant may be thought of by another person as only average. Whether a person is happy or unhappy with their service is essentially a personal experience; no two people have the same perception of what good or bad service means to them. The very personal nature of the customer service experience needs to be accepted by staff working in hospitality and catering organizations right from the outset. If customers are not treated as individuals, they will become disenchanted with the service they receive and may choose to take their business elsewhere.

Although it is not always easy to define exactly what constitutes good service, we are all familiar with circumstances when the level of service we have received is either very good or very bad. In hospitality and catering, the following examples give a flavour of what a good customer service approach is all about and what is considered as bad service.

✪ **In a hotel**: Good service would be when the receptionist remembers the name of a guest's child and the hotel provides a box of toys for the child to play with. Bad service would be not attending to a broken shower in a guest's room immediately.

✪ **In a restaurant**: Good service would be when the management remembers that an evening booking is for a couple's first wedding anniversary and provides a complimentary bottle of champagne. Bad service is when a group telephones in advance to make a booking only to find when they arrive that the waiter has no record of the booking and all the tables are full.

The increasingly competitive nature of the hospitality and catering industry means that organizations are placing more emphasis on customer service than ever before. It is now recognized that maintaining the loyalty of existing customers makes financial sense – it is often claimed that it costs five times as much to get a new customer than it does to retain an existing customer.

By putting in place a well-structured customer service policy, organizations should retain more customers and provide a happier working environment for staff.

Revision questions

1. A pub restaurant wishes to appeal to the pensioners' market.
   Which features are most appropriate?

   (a) A range of discounted alcoholic drinks and take-away food only
   (b) A family room featuring an open fire and a pool table
   (c) A menu featuring spicy finger food and a play area
   (d) A menu featuring value plated food and no-smoking areas   (2 marks)

2. An organization working to quality standards tells all its staff that they must remember their 'internal customers'. This is because:

   (a) Customers who have entered the premises are the most important
   (b) The needs of external customers are best met when the parts of the organization show customer care to each other
   (c) Customers must be dealt with in an informal, friendly way at all times
   (d) Everyone in the organization must work to the same quality standards   (2 marks)

3. What is the most likely measurable result of good customer service?

   (a) Staff turnover will be high
   (b) Word-of-mouth recommendations will increase
   (c) Customers will be easier to satisfy
   (d) Repeat business will be generated   (2 marks)

4. Which is it most important to measure when checking the speed of service in a fast food outlet?

   (a) Number of compliment letters
   (b) Length of time between order and delivery
   (c) Content of compliment letters
   (d) Reductions in room service orders   (2 marks)

5. What is the best reason for evaluating most customer care programmes?

   (a) To ensure the programme is effective and within budget
   (b) To recommend and sell the programme to other companies
   (c) To increase job satisfaction and reduce the budget
   (d) To reduce induction training costs and increase the budget   (2 marks)

Unit 4 key skills

Keys to attainment

These are key skills or aspects of key skills that are central to the Customer Service unit. The key to attainment shows that the relevant aspect of the key skill has also been achieved. You will of course need to develop and practise the key skill during your lessons and in your private studies.

Communication, level 3

When you are:	You should have achieved the following key skills evidence:
Combining information collected from different sources into customer service benchmarks and performance indicators	C3.2 Read and synthesize information from two extended documents about a complex subject. One of these documents should include at least one image. C3.3 Write two different types of documents about complex subjects. One piece of writing should be an extended document and include at least one image.
Demonstrating customer service skills in complex situations	C3.1b Make a presentation about a complex subject, using at least one image to illustrate complex points.

Signposts

These are naturally occurring opportunities for the development of key skills through your learning and assessment. You will not necessarily achieve the signposted key skill through your evidence for the Customer Service unit. You will need to develop additional evidence elsewhere to ensure that you meet the requirements of the key skills units fully.

Communication, level 3

When you are:	There may be opportunities for you to develop the following key skills evidence:
Discussing how to respond to customers using appropriate personal and social skills	C3.1a Contribute to a group discussion about a complex subject.

Information Technology, level 3

When you are:	There may be opportunities for you to develop the following key skills evidence:
Researching customer service standards	IT 3.1 Plan and use different sources to search for and select information required for two different purposes.
Writing to outlets or other sources for information about customer service procedures and practices	IT 3.2 Explore, develop and exchange information and derive new information to meet two different purposes.
Preparing records of practical activities carried out and evaluating customer service standards in two different outlets	IT 3.3 Present information from different sources for two different purposes and audiences. Include at least one example of text, one example of images and one example of numbers.

Improving own learning and performance, level 3

When you are:	There may be opportunities for you to develop the following key skills evidence:
Working on keeping records of your activities and when working on your investigations	LP 3.1, 3.2 and 3.3 – for the activity based requirements over an extended period of time.

Working with others, level 3

When you are:	There may be opportunities for you to develop the following key skills evidence:
Investigating the procedures and practices used to provide customers with quality service standards	WO – for one of the two complex activities required as a minimum. There is a good opportunity for you to carry out a group activity. The activity must include tasks for WO 3.1, 3.2 and 3.3. There is an opportunity for you to work in a small group when collecting information from different sources.

Safety, security and the environment

5

This chapter will help you to learn how safety – including food safety – security and the environment are managed in hospitality and catering outlets.

In this chapter you will learn:

- **about ways of recognizing hazards and controlling risks**

- **how to carry out risk assessments**

- **how to monitor and review workplace safety**

- **about the impact of legislation on employers, staff, customers and others who use outlets**

- **about ways of effectively communicating information about workplace safety**

Maintaining safety, security and environmental protection

Safety, security and environmental issues which affect customers and staff in hospitality and catering include:

- **health and safety**, such as fire prevention, design and layout of workplace areas, handling hazardous substances and manual handling of loads
- **food safety**, such as preventing cross-contamination, maintaining personal hygiene, proper storage, preparation and cleaning methods
- **security**, such as protecting people, property, equipment and materials
- **environmental protection**, such as reducing waste, re-using items, recycling materials, saving energy and water

The implications of maintaining safety, security and environmental protection are all-important and have a bearing on all areas of work in the industry. Safety applies not just to food but also to the environment and people, both customers and staff. It is legally enforced but is also critical to the success of a business.

These issues will impact on:

- **the organization**
- **customers**
- **the staff**
- **the external image of the outlet**
- **the local community**

The organization

Safety, security and concern for the environment are essential to the running of all establishments. Larger establishments now require one member of staff to concentrate on these aspects. Environmental impact has to be considered as well as all the aspects of safety and security required by law and good practice.

Customers

The most important initial requirement of hospitality and catering is for a safe and secure environment in which customers can relax and enjoy their stay and refreshment. This must be planned for and constantly monitored.

The staff

There is a duty in the legislation for all staff, not just management, to be responsible for safety in all workplaces. Security and the protection of the environment are in the interest of all staff and are the personal responsibility of all staff, particularly those who are most often at the establishment.

The external image of the outlet

A breakdown in safety and security will probably be picked up by the press and will have an immediate effect on trade. Prevention is preferable and can be achieved through vigilance, training and monitoring to stop problems occurring.

The local community

Care should be taken to prevent any form of contamination, whether physical, chemical or noise. Contact should be established with the local community so that any concerns expressed can be discussed and dealt with before they become areas of conflict.

Safety in the workplace

There should be a health and safety policy, which provides the basis from which the organization develops its structures and procedures to ensure health and safety. The policy needs to be endorsed by the chief executive. If there are more than five employees in an organization, the policy and the arrangements to carry it out must be recorded in writing.

A health and safety policy should:

✪ **state the values, belief and commitment to health and safety**

✪ **give reasons for best practice in health and safety, i.e. reduced accidents, better working conditions**

✪ **aim to make health and safety matters as important as all other business aims, including profit**

✪ **establish responsibilities for all levels of staff**

✪ **lay down the procedures for full participation in health and safety by all staff, with a specialist who has real time to devote to health and safety issues**

(There is a guide which can be obtained from the Health and Safety Executive on writing a health and safety policy statement.)

Consideration will need to be given to all normal operating situations and to those which only occur spasmodically, i.e. contractors or other non-employees working on the premises, temporary workers.

Communicating information

In an organization there needs to be a culture of safety which must stem from the management and their attitude to it. An example needs to be set of putting safety issues right at the top of the list of priorities rather than tagging them on as a legal nuisance. Communication is essential and for it to be effective all staff should trust and respect for each other and be willing to take responsibility for ensuring safety and security. Too often there is the culture of 'it's not my job'. It is up to management to change this attitude by example and positive interaction with all staff, both giving and receiving respect.

Information about controlling safety, security and the environment needs to be communicated to staff and customers in outlets. Sometimes there are people who may not speak English or understand complicated instructions. Information needs to be communicated clearly and effectively, including:

- identifying what needs to be communicated, such as policies and instructions
- providing workplace safety information appropriate to the audience, such as to managers, operative staff and customers
- matching the communication method to the person, for example speaking, signing, using pictures, videos and CDs
- overcoming barriers to understanding, such as language, culture and reluctance to accept instructions

Good practice for ensuring safety, security and environmental protection

Identifying hazards

As with many other industries, there are a large numbers of hazards in outlets that may cause accidents or ill health to customers and staff. Hazards found in different workplace areas include:

- **food and drink preparation and cooking hazards**, such as leaving spilt water on floors and not separating waste
- **food and drink service hazards**, such as holding food at unsafe temperatures and dealing with physical assaults
- **accommodation service hazards**, such as using faulty vacuum cleaners and handling chemicals improperly
- **reception and front office hazards**, such as handling keys inappropriately and trailing flexes across walkways

The Management of Health and Safety at Work Regulations 1992 require employers to identify the potential hazards which apply in different areas. Some will apply to all areas but others are more likely to occur in certain conditions, for example people can fall on any floor surface but are much more likely to fall on smooth finishes, particularly if they are wet. Having identified this, various strategies can be explored to limit the possibility of occurrence, for example a change to the finish, warning signs, change of practice to limit the possibility of wetting the floor.

Hazard analysis is now required for hygiene in particular, with identification of Critical Control Points (see Figure 5.1, page 176). This sort of identification of hazards can be employed in all areas. Once the CCPs have been identified, appropriate steps can be considered to provide the control needed (see Figure 5.2, page 176).

HACCP
Identify hazards and assess risk
Identify critical control points
Establish limits, tolerances
Monitor control methods
Corrective action
Verification by outsider
Documentation

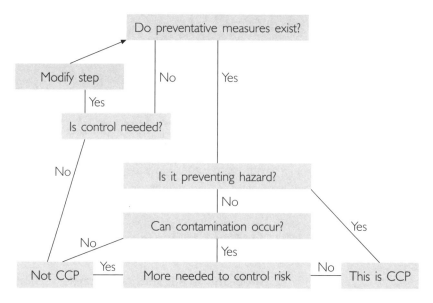

HACCP DECISION TREE

Figure 5.1 *Hazard analysis critical control points*

Effective control of hazards requires:	Comments
Setting standards required	Involving operatives as well as specialists
Communicating these to operatives	In writing plus training and discussion sessions
Measuring performance	Openly and through self appraisal
Corrective action	Complimenting more than criticising Is control method correct?
Constant monitoring through supervision	Responsibility of management

Figure 5.2 *Effective control of hazards*

Controlling hazards

Controls are measures that are carried out to reduce the risk of hazards causing injury or ill health to people and the loss of property. Some common controls which are implemented in different workplace areas include:

✪ **substituting hazardous for less hazardous or biodegradable chemicals**

✪ **breaking large loads into smaller ones**

- using physical controls, such as guards on machines and thermostats in rooms
- keeping records, such as when signing over keys
- good housekeeping, such as removing waste, mopping spills on floors immediately and asking customers to re-use towels
- using safe working methods, such as colour-coded cleaning cloths and chopping boards
- providing training, such as fire prevention and food hygiene
- providing resources, such as staff uniforms and washing facilities

Assessing risks

Following the hazard analysis, it is appropriate to carry out a risk assessment to clarify the severity of the problem (see Figure 5.3).

Identify hazard	Example food mixer
Is item or function necessary?	Yes, in order to produce volume in time-scale
Who is at risk?	Pastry chef and commis, cleaner
What could be the consequences?	Broken limbs: fingers, hands, arms Injuries because of lack of guards Electric shock and fire due to faulty wiring
Control measures	Position food mixer securely where it does not intrude Ensure electrics are tested and to standard Ensure regular maintenance Position warning signs and details of proper use Ensure guards are fitted Only properly trained staff to operate mixer
Record assessment	(Legally required if more than five employees)
Review after changes	i.e. staff training, properly fitting guards, new position, warning notices and details of safe use, regular maintenance and testing of electrics

Figure 5.3 *Possible format for risk assessment*

Risk assessments are the single most important tool in managing safety, security and the environment in outlets. They are used to identify the control measures needed to reduce or prevent risks associated with hazards or reduce inappropriate use of resources. Methods of carrying out risk assessments in workplace areas include:

- **identifying hazards, for example by using visual audits, inspecting records and using checklists**
- **identifying who is at risk of injury and ill health, and inappropriate use of resources**
- **evaluating the levels of risk**
- **deciding if existing control measures are appropriate**

However minor the problem, steps should be taken to avoid the possibility of harm. The following questions should be asked:

- **Is it necessary to carry out the function which presents a hazard? Could the same result be achieved in a different way without the hazard?**
- **What steps can be taken to minimize the risk if the function is essential – safety clothing, guards on machines, warning notices, extra training?**
- **What can be available to alleviate damage if an accident occurs?**

Abbreviation or term	Explanation
Code of practice	Advisory guidelines to develop good practice
COSHH	Control of Substances Hazardous to Health Regulations 1988 (chemicals)
EAW	Electrical Appliances At Work (must be annually inspected for safety and tagged)
EHO	Environmental Health Officer
HACCP	Hazard Analysis Critical Control Points
HASAW	Health and Safety at Work Act 1974 (main legislation covering health and safety)
HSE	Health and Safety Executive
RIDDOR	Reporting Incidents, Diseases and Dangerous Occurrences Regulations 1985

Figure 5.4 *Some health and safety terms*

First aid boxes and trained staff are a legal requirement in establishments over a certain size. The Reporting Incidents, Diseases and Dangerous Occurrences Regulations 1985 (RIDDOR) requires the legal reporting of accidents, some incidents such as explosions, outbreaks of certain diseases, deaths, work related incidents, any injury requiring hospital admittance for more than 24 hours and pathogenic poisoning. The reports should also be used to monitor occurrences and amend procedures.

Maintenance of all equipment and systems should be planned in advance to occur regularly before it becomes necessary, but this will not obviate the need for regular inspection. Some inspections need to be carried out hourly, such as checking the temperature of refrigerators or cleanliness of toilets, others will only need to be done daily or weekly, but nothing should be ignored. There will be a need for corrective maintenance in all establishments, but effective planning should keep this to a minimum and avoid most emergency repairs. When emergency repairs are necessary backup facilities should be available and repairs should be carried out quickly.

By following best practice, and at a minimum European Union Health and Safety Regulations, people's safety will be ensured. Measures include:

✪ **lifting of heavy items with a straight back**

✪ **limiting time spent in front of computer monitors, providing proper seating and possibly foot rests, as well as ergonomic keyboards**

✪ **ensuring first aid boxes are available as well as trained first aiders**

✪ **inspecting electrical appliances annually**

✪ **ensuring the safety of swimming pools etc.**

Monitoring and review procedures

Ways in which supervisory staff in workplaces carry out procedures to monitor the effectiveness of control measures and decide if changes are needed include:

✪ **inspecting operational documents and records, for example accident forms, electricity and water meter readings**

✪ **inspecting staff training and development records**

✪ **observing how staff are following control measures while working**

✪ **inspecting and reporting on records of incidents and accidents**

Figures 5.5–5.8 on pages 180–82 show specimen safety checklists for different areas of an establishment.

Kitchen		√ or ×	Action
Fire	Alarm		
	Extinguishers		
	Smoke alarms		
	Main switches		
	Fire exits		
	Signs		
Hygiene	Sinks		
	Floors, walls, work tops		
	Wash hand basin, soap, brush, drier		
	Cleaning equipment		
	Cleaning chemicals		
	Chemicals stored safely		
	Food stored safely		
	Temperature controls: chilled −5°C hot +63°C		
First aid	Kit		
	Items		
	Incident book		
Maintenance	Electrical safety		
	Equipment working		
	Guards on dangerous machines		
	Instructions on display		
Lighting	Adequate		
Ventilation	Adequate		
	Temperature reasonable		
	Clean vents		
Rubbish	Suitable bins		
	Signs of vermin		

Figure 5.5 *Specimen safety checklist for a kitchen*

Restaurant		√ or ×	Action
Fire	Extinguishers		
	Alarm		
	Signs		
	Exits clear		
Access	Wheelchair		
	Disabled		
Hygiene	Training		
	Personnel		
	Equipment		
	Food storage: chilled −5°C		
	Items		
Ventilation	Temperature		
Maintenance	Electrical		

Figure 5.6 *Specimen safety checklist for a restaurant*

Service area			√ or ×	Action
Fire	Extinguisher	Sited checked		
Safety	Access	Clear		
	Signs	Displayed		
	Electrical			
Hygiene	Wash basin	Soap, drying, nail brush		
	Fridge	Temperature −5°C		
		Space clean		
	Shelves	Items clean		
		Stored safely and correctly		
	Dishwasher	Operating		
		Clean		
	Area clean	Floors, surfaces		

Figure 5.7 *Specimen safety checklist for a service area*

Public areas: toilets, changing rooms and passages		
Passages	**√ or ×**	**Action**
1 Are all lights working?		
2 Do all doors open correctly?		
3 Is the fire exit clear and accessible?		
4 Are the floors clean and dry?		
5 Is fire fighting equipment unobstructed and working?		
6 Are fire alarms clear and working?		
Toilets		
1 Do lights work?		
2 Is all plumbing well maintained?		
3 Are the appliances clean?		
4 Is the floor clean and dry?		
5 Is there an adequate supply of toiletries?		
6 Do all locks work?		
7 Is the bin emptied?		
Changing rooms		
1 Do lights work?		
2 Is the plumbing working?		
3 Is the floor clean and dry?		
4 Are all lockers in good condition?		
5 Are seats safe and stable?		
6 Is the fire exit clear and accessible?		
7 Is the fire alarm accessible and working?		

Figure 5.8 *Specimen safety checklist for public areas*

Legislation

Laws relating to customers

See also pages 134–40.

Hotel Proprietors Act

An 'innkeeper' must provide food, drink and accommodation, if available, to a traveller who appears willing and able to pay and is in a fit state. The Act gives the right of lien (holding guest's property against payment) and deposit holding. A hotel must receive travellers and display a notice to this effect. A hotel's responsibility for guests' belongings is limited unless they are taken for safekeeping (for example, taking a coat to hang up for a customer).

Otherwise the choice of customer is free provided the following Acts are taken into consideration:

- ✪ **Sex Discrimination Act** – it is illegal to discriminate on the grounds of sex
- ✪ **Race Relations Act** – all persons must be treated equally irrespective of race

Contract Law

This concerns agreements that are legally enforceable, not necessarily written. There must be an offer, acceptance and consideration with the intention and capacity to carry out a lawful act. Terms of the agreement may be expressed or implied and any exclusion must be reasonable. The contract should lead to performance unless there is a breach or frustration. For example, coats etc. taken by staff are the responsibility of the establishment.

Guest registration

All guests in hotels must be registered. They must give their name, address and nationality. Guests from outside the EU must also give their passport number and place of issue. The police and Home Office have the right to inspect the register.

Value Added Tax

VAT (17.5 per cent) must be charged on meals, drink and accommodation unless exempted. Customs and Excise Officers have the right of access to the premises at reasonable times.

Supply of Goods and Services Act

Service must be carried out with reasonable care and skill. The price charged must be reasonable.

Sale of Goods Act

Goods sold must be of merchantable quality, i.e. fit for the purpose for which they are sold.

Theft Act

A person who, knowing that payment on the spot is required, dishonestly makes off without paying with intent to avoid payment, is guilty of an offence.

Trade Description Act

It is a criminal offence to give a false or misleading description of a product.

Price Marking Orders

Prices, including VAT and any other charges, must be prominently displayed to customers before a purchase is made.

Weights and Measures

All specified quantities must be accurate.

Officers, often Trading Standards Inspectors, enforce the law and must be allowed access at reasonable times.

Food and Drugs Act

Food must be of the nature, substance and quality that the customer demands.

Laws relating to alcoholic drink

Licensing Acts

A licence is required for selling alcohol in quantities of less than 9 litres.

A licence is issued by licensing magistrates to a person or persons selling alcohol on a premises. The Acts are enforced by police who must be granted access to the premises.

There are three kinds of licence:

✪ **a restaurant (table) licence only is required when serving alcoholic drinks to customers eating a meal.**

✪ **a residential licence is needed to sell alcohol to customers in a residential establishment.**

✪ **an on (full) licence covers the sale of alcohol in restaurants, residential establishments and also in bars.**

Extensions can be gained for special or general occasions, and for the supper hour or longer if there is music and dancing. Occasions must be run properly, with no drunks, drug takers or prostitutes.

The following age limitations apply:

✪ **Those under 14 are not allowed in bars**

✪ **Those under 16 are not allowed to buy or drink alcohol in licensed premises**

✪ **Those between 16 and 18 can drink beer or cider with a meal in licensed premises**

✪ **Those over 18 may purchase, consume, sell and supply alcohol**

Customs and excise

Alcoholic drinks must be sold at the correct alcoholic strength. Customs and excise officers have the right of access to premises and to test samples of alcoholic drinks.

Weights and measures

Beer is sold in pints and half pints and sometimes in metric measures of 250 ml or 500 ml. Measures of other drinks are displayed in ml (spirits are usually 25 ml).

Wine is sold by the glass in measures of 125 or 175 ml. Carafes of wine are 250, 500, 750 or 1000 ml or 9, 10 and 20 floz.

Weights and measures officers have the right of access to the premises and to test samples.

Labelling

Wine-Quality designation, EC Table or Quality QWSPR, VQPRD, legal appellation, labels on alcoholic drinks should include the country of origin, bottler's name and address, alcohol content and volume.

EU wine is either table wine or designated as quality wine, in which case the label should also include the quality QWSPR or VQPRD and the legal name of the wine (see Appendix).

Price marking order

All alcohol sales lists must state the alcoholic content as well as the price including VAT and the measure.

Drink drive limit

If more than 80 mg alcohol is found in the blood, a driver is over the limit.

Laws relating to food hygiene

A wide variety of UK and EU legislation is relevant to the hotel and catering industry. The Food Safety Act 1990 and the Food Hygiene Regulations 1970 are among the most important.

The Food Safety Act 1990

This Act places the responsibility for food safety on staff working at each stage of the food production chain, from the farm to the final point of sale. Staff who handle food are required to have hygiene training.

It is an offence to render food injurious to health or unfit for humans. Under the Act, 'food' refers to almost anything that is eaten, drunk or chewed. For instance, a cup of tea is regarded as food, and so is the water used to make the tea.

According to the legislation, food fails to comply with the food safety requirements:

- ✪ **if it is unfit for human consumption, for example if it contains a cockroach**
- ✪ **if it is so contaminated that it would be unreasonable to expect it to be eaten or drunk in that state**
- ✪ **if it has been made harmful to health by adding something to it or removing something from it, or by using unsuitable handling techniques or processes**
- ✪ **if it is not of the nature, substance or quality demanded by the purchaser, for example a steak pie which contains mostly vegetables with just one or two lumps of meat**
- ✪ **if it is falsely or misleadingly described or presented, for example canned soup served as 'fresh, home-made'**

An Environmental Health Officer can seize food that does not comply with safety requirements, and if necessary serve an improvement notice or close the business. An Environmental Health Officer can also issue an emergency prohibition notice which would mean an establishment could no longer serve food to customers. A court can impose the prohibition.

The Food Hygiene (General) Regulations (1970)

The Regulations ensure that food is protected from contamination by:

- ✪ **raw and cooked food being kept separate during preparation**
- ✪ **open food being covered or effectively screened during sales or delivery**
- ✪ **food handlers using hygienic work methods**
- ✪ **food handlers observing personal hygiene rules**

Food Hygiene Amendments 1995

Foods must be stored below 8°C or above 63°C as appropriate; high risk foods must be stored below 5°C.

Food premises (registration)

All food premises must be registered with the local authority.

Laws relating to health and safety at work

Control of substances hazardous to health

This refers to the correct storage, labelling and usage of cleaning materials and pesticides.

HACCP

Hazard Analysis Critical Control Points is a method of identifying and controlling hazards and risks (see pages 175–6).

Dangerous machines

Machines for slicing etc. must not be used by people under 18 except under supervision. All staff must be trained.

Fire Precautions Act covers areas of warning, fighting, escape, training				
Training	Copy of procedures should be available to all staff	Training to be a minimum of: 2 × 30 mins in first month +30 mins every 6 months if on night duty every 3 months	Exercise every 6 months	
Fire needs	Fuel + heat + air (oxygen)			
Detection	Smoke, flames and/or heat set automatic alarms Manual alarm set off by vigilant staff			
In case of fire	Internal procedures	External (999)		
When alarm is heard	Exit, switch off gas and electrics if possible	Close doors	Report to assembly area	Obey fire marshals
Prevention	No smoking	Check electrics regularly	Store waste and cleaning materials safely	
Signposting	Identify escape routes	Keep fire doors and exits clear and ensure they have signs		

Figure 5.9 *Fire Precautions Act*

Extinguishers

Type	Used on	Dangers
Water, hose,	Wood, paper, fabric	Not on electrics, oil, fat, liquids
Foam	Oils, fat, liquids	Not on electrics
Carbon Dioxide CO2	Electrics, oils, spirits	Not in confined spaces
Halon Gas	Gas, liquids, Electrics	Not in confined spaces
Dry Powder	Gas, liquids, electrics	
Fire Blanket	Fats, oils, people's clothes	

Figure 5.10   *Fire extinguishers*

Fire Precautions Act

This requires an establishment to have fire certificates, exits, notices, and fire fighting equipment and to provide training (see Figures 5.9 and 5.10). This applies to any establishment where there are more than 20 employees on the ground level or more than ten above ground level. Hotels with more than six guests at first floor level, or just one at either second floor level or below ground, must apply for a fire certificate. Inspectors should have access to the premises at reasonable times.

Health and Safety at Work (HSW) Act 1974

It is the duty of every employer to safeguard, so far as is reasonably practicable, the health, safety and welfare of all those in his or her employment. This duty is extended to others who may be affected by the operation of the facility, for example contractors, visitors and members of the general public. In practice the employer must:

- ✪ **ensure that the work environment is regularly monitored in respect of health and safety requirements**
- ✪ **provide plant and equipment which is not a risk to health**
- ✪ **provide safe storage for substances which could pose a threat to safety and ensure their safe use**
- ✪ **provide a written statement of safety policy and bring it to the notice of employees (applies only to those employing five or more staff)**
- ✪ **ensure that work systems and practices are safe**
- ✪ **provide adequate information and training for all**

The HSW Act is not only concerned with regulating the actions of employers. Employees also have a duty under the HSW Act:

- **to take reasonable care to avoid injury to themselves or to others by their work activities**
- **to co-operate with their employers and other agencies to ensure that the requirements of the Act are carried out**
- **not to interfere with or misuse anything provided to protect their health, safety and welfare under the Act**

How is the HSW Act enforced?

The Health and Safety Commission (HSC) and the Health and Safety Executive (HSE) were both established under the HSW Act to provide the framework for publicizing the importance of health and safety and to begin prosecutions for breaches of the Act. The HSC is responsible to the Secretary of State for Employment for taking the necessary steps to secure the health, welfare and safety of people at work and also to protect the public against risks to health and safety arising out of a work situation. The HSE is the operating arm of the HSC and is responsible for enforcing the legislation under the HSW Act.

Inspectors' powers

Inspectors have the right to view staff and examine records to check that the Health and Safety at Work Act is being complied with. Inspectors can also make enquiries into accidents which have occurred at places of employment. This covers accidents not only to employees themselves, but also to visitors, and would include, for example, people using sports centres, hotels, visitor attractions and other leisure and tourism facilities.

If an inspector discovers a contravention of one of the provisions of the HSW Act or any of the earlier legislation that is still in force, the inspector can take one of several courses of action:

- **Improvement notice**: If there is a contravention of any of the requirements of the HSW Act, an improvement notice can be served. This will give a time limit for compliance with the relevant requirement.
- **Prohibition notice**: If the inspector considers that there is a high risk of serious personal injury, a prohibition notice can be issued to put a stop to the activity in question until any specified action to remedy the situation has been completed. The notice can be served on either the person undertaking the activity or the person in control of it.
- **Prosecution**: Over and above the issuing of either a prohibition notice, an improvement notice or both, any person found contravening the Act or any of its regulations is liable to prosecution. Contravention of some of the requirements can lead to prosecution in either the Magistrates' Court

(Sheriffs' Court in Scotland) or the Crown Court in England and Wales (the Sheriffs' Court in Scotland). Either a fine or a term of imprisonment may be imposed depending on the nature of the offence.

✪ **Seizure**: An inspector has the power to seize, render harmless or destroy any substance or article considered to be the cause of imminent danger or serious personal injury.

Premises					Date
Address					Officer
Action	**A** **Nil**	**B** **Minor**	**C** **Major**	**D** **Priority**	**Comments**
1 Food supplies Approved source Delivery checked Stock rotation					
2 Food protection Stored chilled/hot Food handling procedures Ambient storage (DGS) Design/maintenance of equipment and utensils					
3 Premises and Equipment Suitable chemicals used, storage Adequate sinks, machines maintained Storage for cleaned items					
4 Walls, floors, ceilings Cleanliness, repair, construction Adequate lighting					
5 Ventilation Adequate, well designed, clean					
6 Personal hygiene Adequate wash basins and WCs Facilities at wash basins					
7 Refuse disposal Suitable internal facility Suitable external facility, contractor					
8 Pest control Adequate proofing Lift enclosed, clean, maintained					

Figure 5.11 *Specimen inspection sheet used by external inspectors*

Action	A Nil	B Minor	C Major	D Priority	Comments
9 Sanitary facilities Adequate toilets Lit, enclosed, clean, maintained					
10 Personnel Clean, protective clothing as appropriate Jewellery, smoking?					
11 Health and safety First aid kit Machines guarded Electricity at Work Regulations/lift maintenance					
12 Management records Cleaning schedule Temperature records Accident Book/RIDDOR COSHH assessment Safety policy Training records HACCP					

Figure 5.11 *(cont'd)*

Activity 5.1

Legal access

This activity is to make you aware of who has the lawful authority to demand access to premises. List the officials who can demand access legally and give reasons for this.

Activity 5.2

Legal notices and signs

This activity involves identifying legally required notices and signs and then finding them in an establishment of your choice.

1   Using this unit, identify the notices and signs required by law.

2   Highlight those that should be in your chosen establishment.

3   Check that all the notices and signs are displayed in the establishment.

European Directives on health and safety

Six new sets of health and safety at work regulations came into force in the UK on 1 January 1993. They apply to almost all kinds of work activity, including hospitality and catering. Like the health and safety laws that were already in force, they place duties on employers to protect their employees and any other people, including members of the public, who may be affected by their activities.

These new UK regulations were needed to implement six **European Community** (now **European Union**) **Directives** on health and safety at work. The Directives are part of the EU's programme of action on health and safety, which is an essential ingredient in the move towards a single European market. They are also part of a continuing modernization of existing UK law. Most of the duties in the regulations were not completely new but merely clarified existing health and safety legislation. Any hospitality and catering organization which was already complying with the HSW Act and the regulations linked with it would not have found the new regulations at all daunting.

Management of health and safety hazards

Under the Management of Health and Safety at Work Regulations 1992 employers have a duty to carry out risk assessments of their premises in order to highlight potential health and safety risks and to implement positive action to put matters right, thereby reducing the number of accidents in hospitality and catering facilities. Investigators of safety hazards and management have ample evidence to show that accidents are **caused** rather than just happen. Careful investigations of accidents show that many could have been prevented if somebody had taken the time and care to examine the risk potential of the particular building or facility. It may be something as simple as the replacement of a broken floor tile or a cracked window pane. (See pages 211–12 for sources of advice on health and safety measures.)

Hotels and other accommodation

The very diverse nature of the accommodation sector in UK hospitality and catering gives it great appeal to domestic and overseas tourists. Serviced accommodation for business and leisure travellers comes in a vast range of sizes, styles and types – anything from a sixteenth-century half-timbered country house hotel in Herefordshire to a modern 30-storey city-centre hotel. Self-catering accommodation can include cottages, chalets, villas, camping and caravanning. These are particularly popular with families who enjoy the flexibility and value for money which this type of accommodation offers.

From a health and safety point of view, the wide range of accommodation on offer makes a standardized approach to analyzing and eliminating risks quite impossible. The sixteenth-century country house hotel quoted above will have very different health and safety risks associated with it than, say, a caravan site with over 200 pitches.

Potential hazards in both serviced and self-catering accommodation include:

- ✪ **fire (particularly important in high-rise buildings)**
- ✪ **faulty wiring and electrical appliances**
- ✪ **faulty air conditioning**
- ✪ **poorly maintained lifts and elevators**
- ✪ **poor ventilation**
- ✪ **glass doors, screens and windows**
- ✪ **poor lighting**
- ✪ **worn or damaged floor coverings**
- ✪ **blocked corridors**
- ✪ **suspicious packages**

The risk assessments, which are now an essential management function under the new health and safety at work regulations, should highlight such risks and hazards and prompt urgent action by employers. Self-catering accommodation, where by definition the owner or manager of the property may not be on-site, needs very careful attention when it comes to health and safety issues.

Restaurants and other food outlets

There are potential health and safety hazards both for those working in this sector and their customers and clients. Particular examples of risks are:

- **unguarded machinery and kitchen equipment**
- **food stored at the incorrect temperature**
- **dangerous practices involving food preparation**
- **contaminated water supplies**
- **inadequate storage for potentially dangerous cleaning materials**
- **poor lighting**
- **inadequate ventilation**

The Food Safety Act and its associated Food Hygiene Regulations (see pages 186–7) have come about to protect both workers and the public in this area of concern for health and safety.

Food hygiene and safety

Food poisoning

Food poisoning may be defined as follows:

✪ **any disease of an infectious or toxic nature caused by the consumption of food or water**

✪ **all food- and water-borne illnesses**

✪ **illnesses from toxic chemicals**

Food poisoning does not include allergies and food intolerance.

Main causes of food poisoning

Food poisoning may be caused by:

✪ **physical items in food or drink, such as glass, rings, hairs, bolts (which can be seen and felt)**

✪ **chemicals, such as cleaning chemicals**

✪ **dissolved metals, such as mercury from fish, lead from water**

✪ **some foods, such as red kidney beans if not property cooked, some fungi**

✪ **food-borne diseases, such as CJD (BSE), typhoid and some viruses**

✪ **pathogenic bacteria (see Figure 5.12, page 198):**

- **salmonella**   – **staphylococcus aureus**

- **campylobacter**   – **bacillus cereus**

- **clostridium perfringens**   – **clostridium botulinum**

Pathogenic bacteria infect in their own right or produce toxins:

✪ **exotoxins grow on proteins**

✪ **enterotoxins multiply in intestines**

✪ **endotoxins are produced when bacteria are dying**

Food can also be contaminated by:

✪ **moulds**

✪ **yeasts**

Bacteria growth

Bacteria divide into two every 10–12 minutes given the right conditions. In order to grow, bacteria need food (protein) and moisture. Three types of bacteria grow at different temperatures:

- **thermophiles grow fastest at 50–60°C**
- **mesophiles grow fastest at 30–40°C, and also slowly at 10–45°C**
- **psychrophiles grow fastest at 20–30°C, and will also grow at 2°C or above**

Bacteria double every 10–12 minutes, particularly at temperatures of 5–63°C known as the danger zone, as long as food and moisture are available. Bacteria cannot live in a high acid or alkaline environment.

Some bacteria become spores which have thick self-protecting walls, for example bacillus cereus. They are therefore not killed off by heat or chemicals and, given the right conditions, can revert to being pathogenic bacteria.

What can be done to minimize the risk of food poisoning

Good design and maintenance of premises and equipment are essential to minimize the risk of food poisoning.

Site selection

The site selected for the premises should not be near any possible sources of contamination. A clean water supply should be available, as well as facilities for safe sewage and waste disposal.

Design of premises

There should be physical barriers between the separate functions of catering organizations with a logical workflow between them. The amount of space for each function should be adequate. Control at each stage will help to prevent hazards. It should be easy to clean the premises and keep out pests. Separate storage areas should be provided for each sort of food. Hygiene facilities should be available for staff.

Adequate ventilation requires 15 air changes per hour. Screened openings should be provided for natural ventilation. Filters used for air extraction should be easy to clean as they will trap grease.

Bacterium	Incubation	Symptoms	Source	Remarks
Bacillus cereus	1–9 hrs	Toxin nausea	Cereals, rice	Found in cooked food
Bacillus cereus	8–12 hrs	Toxin diarrhoea	Cereals, rice	At room temp.
Campylobacter	3–5 days	Fever, diarrhoea, vomiting	Animals	Found in raw milk, unclean water
Clostridium botulinum	2 hrs–2 days	Toxin causing paralysis/death	Intestines, soil	Anaerobic, found in canned foods
Clostridium perfringens	8–18 hrs	Mild diarrhoea for 24 hrs	Soil, gut	Spores, found in reheated stews
Salmonella	6 hrs–3 days	Vomiting, diarrhoea	Gut, poultry and pets are carriers	Cross-contamination
Staphylococcus aureus	2–6 hrs	Vomiting 24–48 hrs	Humans, cow udders	Caused by food handling
Illness				
Dysentery	4 days	Diarrhoea, fever, nausea, 4–7 days	Carried in human faeces	Cross-contamination
E. (Escherichia) Coli	2 days	Bloody diarrhoea, leads to renal failure	Animal intestines	Found in undercooked mince, raw milk
Typhoid (enteric fever)	1–3 wks	Headache, fever malaise, death	Carried by humans	Cross-contamination to shellfish
Gastro-Enteritis, viral	12–72 hrs	Fever, vomiting, diarrhoea	Bivalve molluscan shellfish	Found in shellfish

Example				
	Number of people infected	**Symptoms**	**Cause**	**Remarks**
Salmonella	19	Diarrhoea	Cold 'cooked' turkey	Heated to 57–60°C rather than 72°C

Figure 5.12 *Bacteria which cause food poisoning*

Ventilation should allow air to pass from cleaner areas to dirtier areas. There should be adequate space for ventilation around motors and condensors.

For food prep areas 540 lux of natural and artificial light is required.

Construction features should be solid with no corners, for example:

- ✪ **Floors should have granolithic, terrazzo or specialist finishes**
- ✪ **Walls should be made of thermoplastic vinyl sheets, or concrete coated with epoxy resin or rubber paint**
- ✪ **Ceilings – if they are hollow there needs to be ease of access for cleaning and maintenance**
- ✪ **Surfaces should be non-absorbent and should resist heat, chemicals and liquids and have bumper bars**
- ✪ **Drainage should be provided by sloping floors, gulleys, traps and grease traps**
- ✪ **Colours should be light**
- ✪ **Doors should open wide, be self-closing, fit closely and be durable and easily cleaned**

Facilities

The hot water supply should be continuous. The cold water supply should be separate from the drinking water supply, which should come direct from the mains. Sanitary and changing facilities should be separate from food areas. Wash hand basins should be provided with a notice to wash hands.

Equipment for waste disposal includes waste disposers, waterproof sacks, plastic or metal bins and compactors. There should be a separate refuse collection area.

Equipment

Equipment should be suitable for catering. For ease of cleaning, equipment should be mobile, coloured according to usage and have a smooth finish with no corners. Stainless steel is the ideal material.

Notices giving details of correct usage of equipment and any particular risks should be displayed. Maintenance schedules should be kept.

Cleaning

The purpose of cleaning is to ensure premises are hygienic and have an attractive appearance and also to obey legal requirements.

Cleaning schedules

Cleaning schedules should include:

- ✪ **what is to be cleaned**
- ✪ **how the cleaning is to be carried out**
- ✪ **when and how often the area is to be cleaned**

- who will carry out the cleaning
- how much time is needed
- what clothing is to be worn
- what materials and chemicals are to be used
- what precautions need to be taken

The supervisor will be responsible for the operation.

Cleaning agents

The Control of Substances Hazardous to Health Regulations 1988 require that cleaning agents are stored separately. It is important not to mix chemicals.

Detergents emulsify grease and need to be mildly alkaline. They act by wetting, emulsifying, saponifying and softening water. Disinfectants reduce bacteria to a safe level. They should be quick acting and capable of killing off a wide range of bacteria. Sanitizers are a detergent and disinfectant combined. Acids remove scale and alkalines are used to clean ovens.

Soap should be available for washing hands.

Activity 5.3

Mr Brown, the purchasing manager, has decided to change the company the hotel uses for the supply of cleaning materials. The new supplier offers a broad range of cleaning materials and equipment, which will be used throughout the establishment. The new supplier has agreed to supply the hotel with notices and signs, which can be used around the hotel to ensure that safe practices are used when handling the cleaning materials.

Mr Brown has asked you to produce a list for him of the signs that will be needed for each department and for the central store area.

Cleaning and disinfecting methods

Cleaning should be carried out in six stages:

1 **preclean**
2 **main clean with detergent at 55°C**
3 **rinse**

4   disinfect for two minutes

5   final rinse at 80°C

6   dry by evaporation

Two sinks should be used, one for detergent and one for disinfectant. Alternatively a machine may be used.

Safe storage

Stock should be rotated on a first in first out (FIFO) basis, taking account of the 'use by' and 'best by' date markings. Storage facilities should be cleaned to deter pests and prevent contamination. The environment should be cool and dry to minimize deterioration of food. Cleaning and hazardous materials should be stored separately.

The delivery point should be clean. When foods are delivered they should be transferred to their place of storage as soon as possible. The purchase specification and date codes should be checked to ensure food is fresh. Foods should be free from obvious contamination. Frozen foods should be below −13°C and chilled foods below 8°C or 5°C. Containers to store items should be clean.

Dry food should be stored in sealed bins off the floor. Cans should not be dented or blown. The length of time canned food may be kept varies, for example canned fruit may be kept for up to nine months.

Hot foods should be stored at above 63°C, or small quantities should be recooked to a temperature of 70°C. The temperature and storage time should be checked – the maximum storage time for cooked foods is one and a half hours.

Chilled foods should be stored at below 2–5°C for a maximum of two days, frozen foods at below −18°C and ice cream that is about to be served at −7°C.

Food Spoilage

Food spoilage is caused by:

- ✪ **the growth of living things:**
    - **bacteria – clostridium, acetobacter, lactobacillus, streptococcus**
    - **moulds – botrytis, penicillium**
    - **yeasts on jams, cheese, wine, etc.**
- ✪ **oxidation, which causes browning and makes food rancid**
- ✪ **enzyme reactions which cause browning of potatoes and apples, and discoloration of unblanched vegetables**

Food preservation

Food is preserved to kill micro-organisms and prevent the growth of microbes.

The following methods are used:

- ✪ **chilling – for a maximum of two or three days as psychrophiles may be growing**
- ✪ ***sous-vide* – food is cooked, vacuum sealed and then chilled; it may be kept for 21 days**
- ✪ **capkold – similar to *sous-vide*, this method is used for bulk quantities**
- ✪ **freezing – blast freezing at 30 mph to a temperature of –30°C, plate or immersion freezing or cryogenic freezing in gas**
- ✪ **reducing the moisture – by accelerated freeze drying (AFD), sun drying, air drying by machine or adding salt or sugar**
- ✪ **vacuum packing**
- ✪ **using chemicals such as sulphur dioxide, sodium nitrate, acids (vinegar)**
- ✪ **smoking**
- ✪ **irradiation**
- ✪ **heat treatment:**
  - **– pasteurization – food is heated to 65°C which kills pathogens but not spoilage bacteria**
  - **– ultra heat treated (UHT) – food is heated to 100°C which kills pathogens and spoilage bacteria but not spores**
  - **– sterilization – food is heated to 100°C for longer which kills pathogens, spoilage bacteria and spores**
- ✪ **canning, which provides a vacuum seal (any blown or dented cans should be eliminated)**

This needs to cover ensuring the safety and protection from damage or loss of:

- ✪ **people – staff, customers and any persons in the premises**
- ✪ **property – the building, equipment, stock, personal items**
- ✪ **money – takings, floats, personal money, cash and money transfers**
- ✪ **information – business records, personal data**

The Health and Safety at Work Act makes it a legal duty for an employer to be responsible for the safety and welfare of those in a workplace. In a hospitality establishment the guest will expect to be in a protected environment. Staff need to be made aware of potential risks and procedures need to be put in place to anticipate problems (see Figure 5.13, page 204).

The police will offer advice on crime prevention. Panic and alarm systems, which directly connect with the local police, should be installed. There are also Business Watch schemes in localities, for example Pub Watch, Restaurant Watch etc., which provide the opportunity to compare good practice and exchange information regarding:

- ✪ **customers who have caused problems – they can be identified with the help of photographs from security cameras and can then be excluded from other establishments**
- ✪ **staff who have been dismissed**
- ✪ **equipment which could be purchased jointly**

These schemes provide a forum for advice and training initiatives from police and other specialists.

Security of	Premises	Design is important access should be limited
	Keys	Control master keys and computerized key cards
	Stock	Should be controlled and recorded, deliveries checked, orders and requisitions signed by authorized staff and goods issued only against a requisition
		External stocktaking should be used
	Payment	Non-payment for service or goods is a theft; obtain updated list of known customers who have not paid bills from finance houses and 'Business Watch'
	Money	Secure payment points, sign for float (change), detect forgeries
		Other forms of payment: cheques, cards, EPTOS
Legal responsibility?	Guests' belongings	Provide safe deposit boxes for valuables
	Staff	Take responsibility on behalf of establishment
	Lost property	Hotel Proprietor's Act – a record must be kept of lost property which must be retained for three months
Methods	Identification	Badges
	CCTV	To detect suspicious behaviour
	Alarms, scanners	Check regularly, connect to police
	Staff	Should be vigilant, aware, responsible, empowered
		Should be trained in safety procedures, with frequent updates
		Involve all staff in risk assessments
		All staff need to be made aware of procedures
Special concerns	Bombs	Look out for suspicious bags, etc.
	Violence	Be firm and polite
	Drug abuse	Be alert
	Death	Call doctor and police, be discreet

Figure 5.13 *Security in hospitality and catering*

Protecting the environment

There is an expanding requirement on businesses to be aware of their responsibilities for the environment, both local and globally. This requires a much greater emphasis on assessment of the impact that the outlet is going to have on the environment.

The first step is to develop a culture of environment consciousness within the establishment with all staff being involved and committed to improving the impact the outlet has environmentally. This will require resources being invested, which will only show benefit in monetary terms over a very long term, if at all. Whenever a decision is to be made, its environmental impact must be considered. Figure 5.14 on page 206 shows a framework for carrying out an environmental audit.

Waste management

Recycling should be given strong emphasis. Whenever possible, environmentally-friendly items that do not create waste should be used.

The following steps should be taken to reduce the amount of waste:

- **glass – the recycling of broken glass and glass containers is now much more common and should be automatic in all catering outlets, particularly licensed ones**
- **paper – recycled paper products should be used wherever possible; paper from offices and customer areas should be reused as scrap and then recycled**
- **plastics – use of plastics should be limited to those which can be recycled or will break down**
- **food – compostable matter should be separated and used for animal consumption**
- **liquid – care should be taken to ensure that grease and fats are separated and disposed of as solid food waste; the quantity of liquid used should be reduced where hygienically possible and all water outlets should be controlled**
- **other items – equipment should be considered for reuse, if not in house then possibly for charitable efforts, which will benefit others, limit waste and be good publicity**

Environmental audit of			
	Control	*Effectiveness*	*Recommendations*
Energy Lighting Heating Ventilation Controls			
Water Uses Pipework			
Air Pollution Ventilation			
Noise External Internal			
Hazards Safety precautions Signs			
Purchasing			
Waste Glass Paper Plastics Food Liquid Other Items			
Comments			Date Signature

Figure 5.14 *Framework for carrying out an environmental audit*

Energy conservation

Energy is an expensive requirement that needs to be monitored for continued effectiveness.

An audit should be carried out to ascertain what is needed in different areas. The following questions could be asked:

✪ **Are guests and staff comfortable with lighting, heating/air conditioning?**

- ✪ **Could insulation and other waste reduction methods be better employed?**
- ✪ **Could there be greater controls on the amount of energy used, for example by using energy saving lighting?**
- ✪ **Could more efficient methods get the same or better results? Staff as well as experts should be asked and a comparison made with similar establishments. It might be possible to recycle energy.**

Water quality and conservation

The following will conserve water and ensure water quality:

- ✪ **inspecting the water and drainage system on a regular basis**
- ✪ **having complete plans of the system**
- ✪ **testing water at critical points to ensure it is safe and there are no possibilities for pollution**
- ✪ **replacing old pipework**
- ✪ **considering new advances in purification to limiting the use of more harmful chemicals**
- ✪ **recycling, including using waste or rain water for garden irrigation or flushing toilets**

Purchasing responsibly

Purchasing responsibly includes:

- ✪ **buying quality and controlling stock levels**
- ✪ **evaluating all requirements carefully**
- ✪ **considering local sourcing and bulk purchasing**
- ✪ **buying recycled and environmentally-friendly products**
- ✪ **renting when appropriate instead of buying**
- ✪ **avoiding disposables, plastics and overpackaged goods**

Air quality and emissions

Air quality can be evaluated by sampling and by considering the comments and opinions of staff and customers. Pollution, for example, smoke, chemicals, humidity, should be minimized. Natural and mechanical ventilation needs monitoring and updating if necessary.

Noise monitoring and limitation

Noise is now recognized as a health and safety issue and is controlled by Environmental Health Officers. Traffic is an example of an external source of noise. Internal sources include plumbing, doors, other guests, television, functions, bars, etc. Action should be taken to limit the sources of noise through better design and regular maintenance. Insulation could be increased to ensure the peace and quiet wanted for sleep in particular.

Supervising, monitoring and managing safety, security and the environment

There is a constant need to ensure that at each stage of the operation safety, security and the environment are given top priority. It is not sufficient to train staff and set up systems – they must be constantly monitored and any possible changes considered.

Checklists should be provided for each area. When they have been completed they should be filed and any concerns reported, recorded and actioned. Complacency is the most dangerous attitude and all areas, even those considered at very low risk, should be monitored.

Communication is essential to ensure that staff not only fulfil the legal requirements for induction and training but also understand and carry out their role with regard to safety, security and the environment.

Monitoring and recording will ensure that the tasks and checks are performed, that any discrepancies are reported and appropriate action is taken, and that the action leads to improved performance. Supervision is required to ensure this is carried out effectively.

Management must set a good example at all times and take time to consider concerns arising from the monitoring. They should look around the entire establishment themselves and try out the staff toilets and the canteen.

Some records must be kept by law, for example accident reports; others, such as records of equipment breakdown and maintenance, are very useful management tools to assess use and possible replacement.

Figure 5.15 on page 210 provides a framework for monitoring and reviewing safety at an establishment.

Evaluation of safety at		
By		on
Strengths	**Criteria**	**Weaknesses**
	Meeting requirements Standards Customers Special needs	
	Complying with legal requirements Hygiene Safety Licensing	
	Organization Staff Communications	
	Staff performance Knowledge	
	Dealing with the unforeseen	
Reliable/Valid	**Data collection methods**	**Unreliable**
	Safety, security and environmental report forms	
	Accident and incident report forms	
	Staff training records	
	Observing staff following control measures	
Recommendations for improvements		
Policy		
Facility		
Staff		
Are recommendations	Relevant Yes/No	Cost-effective Yes/No
Comments		

Figure 5.15 *Framework for evaluating safety*

Information sources

You should make use of work experience or part-time jobs as sources of information. It will be particularly useful to note how health, safety, hygiene, security and environmental protection information is given to first level staff.

Visiting speakers or site visits will provide interest and additional insights.

For example:

✪ **The local environmental health department may be able to provide guidance on the standards they expect organizations and outlets within their authority to maintain**

✪ **A manager from a licensed premise's outlet or the housekeeper from an accommodation outlet could talk about how manual handling hazards are controlled**

✪ **A representative from a contract catering company could talk about the company's approach to hazard analysis**

A representative from the local police force or a shopping centre may be able to speak about appropriate security risks and controls including topics like CCTV, 'shopwatch' or 'pubwatch' networks. The premises manager within the centre may be able to provide details of waste, energy and water control measures and show the cost benefits of effective measures. Speakers from organizations such as Friends of the Earth may be able to provide a useful insight into 'green' facilities management.

You could collect different organizational procedures, such as accident books, health and safety leaflets and food monitoring records. Drawings of organizational charts may be an effective way to show the lines of authority for control, monitoring and review. Copies of reports from newspapers or trade journals may be useful for providing real examples of non-compliance.

Sources of advice on health and safety measures

✪ **The Health and Safety Executive**: The HSE has a network of regional offices covering England, Scotland and Wales with staff who can advise on all issues relating to health and safety at work (Northern Ireland has a separate Health and Safety Agency which, although independent of the HSE, liaises closely with it on matters of mutual interest). The HSE operates a public enquiry service from its Sheffield offices, offering advice and information on a wide range of health and safety issues. The HSE produces a wide range of leaflets on health and safety and will advise on the implementation of the HSW Act and the regulations produced as a result of EU Directives on health and safety.

✪ **Environmental Health Department**: Operated by the local authority, this department is a good source of advice on such issues as noise pollution and control, food hygiene and safety, the EU Package Travel Directive and COSHH.

✪ **Fire Authority**: The local fire authority offers safety information and advice and is the body responsible for issuing fire certificates. It can advise on the purchase of fire safety equipment and training for staff in its use.

✪ **Building Control Department**: Often part of the local authority planning department, building control staff can give advice on the building regulations, many of which contain instructions on the use of certain building materials and techniques to reduce fire risks and improve safety and security generally.

✪ **Health and safety consultants**: In view of the growing amount and complexity of legislation concerning health and safety, specialist consultants can be employed to advise on particular health and safety issues, for example in relation to the regulations brought about by the EU Directives. Consultancies vary enormously in size and style of operation, but there are certain points which an organization must bear in mind when selecting a consultant, such as competence and cost. The HSE can supply an information leaflet on the subject, entitled *Selecting a Health and Safety Consultancy*.

✪ **Professional bodies**: These are helpful in providing advice and publications relating to health and safety. One example is the Hotel, Catering and Institutional Management Association (HCIMA).

✪ **Universities and colleges**: These often put on courses concerning health and safety issues and may offer consultancy services themselves.

✪ **Industrial training boards**: Some industries have training boards, for example the Hotel and Catering Training Board (HCTB), which are active in assessing training needs in health and safety and organizing courses.

✪ **Solicitors and advice centres**: As with any legal matters, solicitors, the Citizens' Advice Bureau and local legal advice centres can give advice on the legislation relating to health and safety, as well as suggesting sources of further advice and information.

✪ **Internet and CD-ROM**: Your school or college library will have internet and perhaps CD-ROM facilities which will be useful when researching sources of advice.

Revision questions

1   Cleaning is best described as:

    (a)   Destruction of all harmful germs
    (b)   Making an area fresh and attractive
    (c)   Washing away harmful substances
    (d)   Removal of all unwanted material
                                    (2 marks)

2   When storing water-based emulsions, which one of the following should be avoided?

    (a)   High humidity
    (b)   Normal room temperature
    (c)   Well ventilated areas
    (d)   Freezing conditions   (2 marks)

3   The basic reason for the provision of fire equipment is to:

    (a)   Satisfy the insurance requirements
    (b)   Control a local fire
    (c)   Give reassurance to the occupants
    (d)   Reduce the amount of assistance needed from the fire brigade
                                    (2 marks)

4   When is a fire certificate issued by the local fire authority?

    (a)   When all staff have passed the authority's fire safety tests
    (b)   When the authority is satisfied adequate precautions have been taken
    (c)   When all management have passed the authority's fire safety test
    (d)   When the authority is satisfied with the fire warnings system   (2 marks)

5   Which is most important to maintain hygiene standards?

    (a)   Hygiene policy is displayed
    (b)   Staff are suitably trained
    (c)   An Environmental Health Officer is contacted
    (d)   Kitchen cleaning schedules are devised
                                    (2 marks)

6   An 'improvement notice' is an official instruction. Which problem could it relate to?

    (a)   Drinking after hours
    (b)   Not cleaning the kitchens properly
    (c)   Not paying bills quickly
    (d)   Allowing under-age persons in the bar
                                    (2 marks)

7   Where is a fire blanket most likely to be required?

    (a)   Boiler house
    (b)   Reception
    (c)   Beer cellar
    (d)   Kitchen   (2 marks)

8   Frozen foods should be stored at:

    (a)   Below 13°C
    (b)   Below −13°C
    (c)   Below 3°C
    (d)   Below −10°C   (2 marks)

Unit 5 key skills

Keys to attainment

These are key skills or aspects of key skills that are central to the Safety, Security and the Environment unit. The key to attainment shows that the relevant aspect of the key skill has also been achieved. You will of course need to develop and practise the key skill during your lessons and in your private studies.

Communication, level 3

When you are:	You should have achieved the following key skills evidence:
Investigating hazards, controls and monitoring and reviewing procedures	C3.2 Read and synthesize information from two extended documents about a complex subject. One of these documents should include at least one image.
Presenting information to a range of people using at least three methods of communication	C3.1b Make a presentation about a complex subject, using at least one image to illustrate complex points. C3.3 Write two different types of documents about complex subjects. One piece of writing should be an extended document and include at least one image.

Signposts

These are naturally occurring opportunities for the development of key skills through your learning and assessment. You will not necessarily achieve the signposted key skill through your evidence for the Safety, Security and the Environment unit. You will need to develop additional evidence elsewhere to ensure that you meet the requirements of the key skills units fully.

Application of number, level 3

When you are:	There may be opportunities for you to develop the following key skills evidence:
Analyzing accident data	N3.1 Plan and interpret information gained from two different types of sources, including a large data set. N3.2 Carry out multi-stage calculations to do with: A amounts and sizes B scales and proportion C handling statistics D rearranging and using formulae Work with a large data set on at least one occasion. N3.3 Interpret results of calculations, present findings and justify methods of interpretation. Use at least one graph, one chart and one diagram.

Communication, level 3

When you are:	There may be opportunities for you to develop the following key skills evidence:
Feeding back to others in the group regarding the methods used to communicate information about health and safety	C3.1a Contribute to a group discussion about a complex subject.

Information Technology, level 3

When you are:	There may be opportunities for you to develop the following key skills evidence:
Searching the internet and CD-ROMs for information	IT3.1 Plan and use different sources to search for and select information required for two different purposes.
Using information from a downloadable resource to print out and include either as extracts or complete in your work	IT3.2 Explore, develop and exchange information and derive new information to meet two different purposes.
Presenting information to a range of people using at least three methods of communication	IT 3.3 Present information from different sources for two different purposes and audiences. Include at least one example of text, one example of images and one example of numbers.

Purchasing, costing and control

6

This unit will help you understand the importance of purchasing costing and control in the daily operations of hospitality and catering outlets, and assist you in learning about the principles and methods that are used by successful outlets. You will also learn that knowledge and skills in this important area are required by all levels of staff with financial responsibilities in an outlet, such as supervisors, departmental heads and managers.

In this unit you will learn:

- **about the methods of purchasing the various goods and services used by different departments**

- **about different sources of supply and the necessary systems of documentation and records**

- **about the importance of correct methods of receiving, storing and issuing goods**

- **why and how resources must be controlled**

- **how the cost and selling price of simple and complex products can be calculated**

- **about the preparation and use of costing and sales information**

Purchasing and control in outlets

A wide range of resources are required by an organization within the hospitality and catering industry to carry out its business. All organizations that are involved in providing food and drink will need to purchase the raw ingredients and the relevant equipment to convert the raw ingredients to products (for example stoves, mixers), as well as storage facilities. In addition, there are many other products which are used daily when providing food or drink. These include cleaning and packaging equipment. Staffing is also a resource – the numbers employed will depend on the size and complexity of the organization.

Every area or sector of the hospitality and catering industry is involved in purchasing. In this section of the unit we will explore sources of supply and purchasing methods. We will also examine the different stages in the purchasing process (the purchasing cycle), the responsibilities of the purchaser and the various control methods used.

The hospitality and catering industry has a very close relationship with the food supply industry. It follows that whatever affects the food supply industry will directly affect the hotel and catering industry. Recent examples of this include the issue of BSE and the banning of the sale of beef on the bone for a period of time.

When and where it is practicable, all sources of supply should be investigated. The person responsible for purchasing should constantly be striving to find new suppliers. In most towns there will be several wholesale greengrocers and butchers, cash and carry warehouses, etc., all of whom are potential suppliers. Many catering outlets like to use local produce as far as possible and promote local specialities, for example special sausages or local duck. There is increased use of organic ingredients and many catering establishments will seek out local suppliers of organic produce.

It might be preferable to use the minimum number of suppliers, thereby minimizing search costs, time and uncertainty. Some sort of selection procedure is then needed in order to identify those who are to become regular suppliers.

Large establishments with high volume purchase requirements usually invite suppliers to submit tenders for the supply contract. The catering company draws up detailed specifications of all its product requirements and asks suppliers to 'bid' for the contract. The tendering documents will also include information on frequency of delivery, credit arrangements, etc. On receipt of the tenders, the catering company chooses the cheapest option (so long as all the suppliers are trustworthy and reliable) and agrees a contract with the supplier for certain products for a period of time, generally 3–12 months.

Hospital catering		Fast food outlet	
1	Maintain quality	1	Maintain quality
2	Minimize costs	2	Maintain competitive position
3	Assure regular supplies	3	Minimize costs
4	Minimize investment	4	Minimize investment
5	Maintain competitive position	5	Assure regular supplies

Figure 6.1 *Comparison of likely priorities in two different sectors of the industry*

The purchasing function

To achieve quality, five basic steps need to be carried out, each associated with the purchasing function:

1 **write purchase specifications**

2 **appraise suppliers**

3 **select supplier**

4 **place the order**

5 **inspect the delivery**

All these activities need to be placed in the context of the objectives of the purchasing function. In addition to maintaining quality, the manager will probably have to obtain the lowest possible purchase price, minimize investment and make sure that the commodities and supplies are always available (with the exception of seasonal produce).

Each sector of the hospitality and catering industry will have different priorities. Two examples can be seen in Figure 6.1.

Purchase specifications

Most catering operations will use the concept of purchase specifications. Small establishments may not have written specifications but the manager or owner will have a preference for a certain brand of product. In large establishments where commodities are supplied in bulk, the purchase specification may be extensive and detailed. The purpose of having a purchase specification is twofold: it helps to assure quality and it is a management tool. Information contained within a purchase specification can include:

✪ **intended use of product**

✪ **name of product**

- ✪ type, grade, brand
- ✪ size, weight
- ✪ minimum and maximum order parameters
- ✪ cost parameters
- ✪ applicable legislation standards
- ✪ edible yield
- ✪ packaging
- ✪ inspection procedure on delivery
- ✪ supply procedures
- ✪ delivery times and frequencies

There are both advantages and disadvantages of using a purchase specification:

- ✪ **Advantages**
  - – **It ensures lowest cost of supply while maintaining quality**
  - – **It ensures raw materials match the process, for example the right size and grade of chips for a deep fat fryer**
  - – **If facilitates contractual agreements and eliminates misunderstandings**
- ✪ **Disadvantages**
  - – **It is costly to draw up initially**
  - – **It can cause rigidity in making the purchasing decision**
  - – **It can be too vague or too rigorous**

Alternatively, the catering company can select a list of nominated suppliers from which products can be purchased. This system is much more flexible than using contracted suppliers and allows the manager some choice as to which supplier to use at any one time. Commodity prices may fluctuate since the caterer will be paying the current market price as opposed to a fixed contract price, but the caterer is now able to switch from a poor supplier to a new supplier much more quickly.

Stages in the purchasing process

Whatever the product purchased, whether food, liquor, cleaning materials, beds or ovens, the same stages will occur in the purchasing process. Many organizations refer to the purchasing process as the purchasing cycle. Figure 6.2 on page 222 shows the stages in the purchasing process.

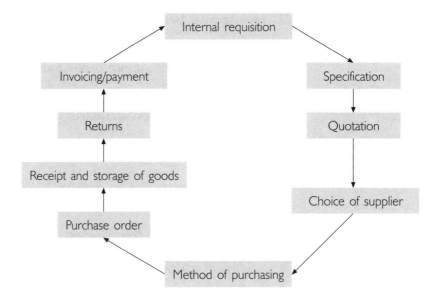

Figure 6.2 *Stages in the purchasing process*

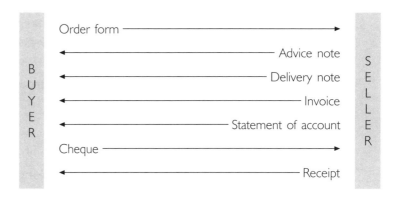

Figure 6.3 *Flow of business documents*

Documentation used in purchasing

Figure 6.3 shows the generally accepted documents which flow between the buyer and the seller. The direction of the arrows indicates the flow of the documents.

Order form

After receiving a price list from the supplier (the seller), the buyer will send out an order form (see Figure 6.4). This will include:

✪ **the name, address and telephone number of the buyer's business**

ORDER			
From	Majestic Hotel Main Road Brighton East Sussex BN1 3AB	Tel 01234 567890 Fax 01234 567899 purchasing@majestic.brighton.co.uk www.majestic-brighton.co.uk	Order no. *5654* Date *13/02/01*
To	Comfort Bedding Peak Industrial Estate Newtown Lancs LA5 9OP		

PLEASE SUPPLY

Quantity	Description	Your ref. no.	Price each
25	135 × 190 cm divan beds	123456	£185.00

Delivered by: *Road*

To: *The above address*

Signature of approval: *Samantha Bradley* Buyer

Figure 6.4   *Order form*

- ✪ **the name and address of the seller's business**
- ✪ **a reference number to which both buyer and seller can refer**
- ✪ **the quantity, description, seller's catalogue number and price of the items required**
- ✪ **the delivery address (this is important as goods may need to be sent to a branch rather than to the invoice address)**
- ✪ **a signature by someone who is authorized to approve the purchase**

Once the supplier has received the order form, that company will:

- ✪ **check with the stores department to see if the goods are in stock**
- ✪ **inform the production department if the goods have to be made**
- ✪ **inform the distribution department if they have to be delivered**
- ✪ **inform the accounts department so that an invoice can be made out**

Did You Know?

As part of the credit control system, a buyer may be checked for creditworthiness prior to processing the order.

```
                        DELIVERY NOTE

                        Comfort Bedding
                     Peak Industrial Estate
                          Newtown
                          Lancashire
                          LA5 9OP

    Tel 01567 123456
    Fax 01567 123457                          sales@comfort-bedding.co.uk
                                              www.comfort-bedding.co.uk

    Invoice To      Majestic Hotel      Deliver To      Majestic Hotel
                    Main Road                           Main Road
                    Brighton                            Brighton
                    East Sussex                         East Sussex
                    BN1 3AB                             BN1 3AB

    Your order no. 5654
    Delivery note no. 19873                  Date 19 February 2001

    Quantity    Description      Ref. no.    Price/unit    Delivery date

    25          135 X 190 cm     123456      £185.00       28/02/01
                divan beds

    Goods Received by: M Philpott

    Position: Storekeeper

    Signature: Mark Philpott

    Payment authorized by:                   Date:
```

Figure 6.5 *Delivery note*

Advice/despatch note

Once the buyer has been found to be satisfactory in terms of
creditworthiness, the supplier may send out an advice note. This generally
contains the same information as the delivery note (see below) and states
when the goods are to be delivered.

Delivery note

The delivery note (see Figure 6.5) is often similar in layout to the advice note
and invoice. It is usually packed in with the goods. When the buyer unpacks
the items a check can be made to see if the stated items have been received
in an undamaged condition.

When the goods are delivered by the seller's own vehicle, the driver will be given a copy of the delivery note and will ask the buyer (or the person receiving the goods) to sign for the goods. This is to confirm that the goods have been delivered.

Goods received note

Within the buying organization it is important to have a system for recording and checking all goods which are delivered to the organization. Once the goods are delivered and have been checked to see if they are in good condition, it is normal procedure to produce a goods received note. This is an internal document that notifies other departments that the goods have been accepted in good condition.

Once checked, the goods are either put into stock or sent to production. The goods received note is usually produced in triplicate: one copy is held by the goods received department, one is passed to the purchasing department and one is passed to the accounts department for processing.

Sales invoice

The seller (supplier) will now bill the buyer using a sales invoice (see Figure 6.6, page 226). This is the demand for payment of goods supplied. The invoice will state:

- **the tax date**
- **the goods or services supplied**
- **the quantity supplied**
- **the cost of each item**
- **any VAT added**
- **any discounts being offered (e.g. for prompt payment)**
- **the total cost payable by the buyer (purchaser) to the seller**
- **'E & OE' (errors and omissions excepted)**

Invoices are very important legal and financial documents. The selling organization, if VAT registered, must state its VAT registration number on the invoice. Both buying and selling organizations must keep all invoices for five years as they are often checked by auditors, the Inland Revenue and HM Customs and Excise (for VAT).

The accounts department in the selling organization will: record the amount of the sale and the name of the debtor in the sales ledger and record the value of the goods sold in a sales account.

The buyer will check the invoice against the original order form and goods received note to see if they all agree. If they do, then payment will be

```
                        INVOICE

                    Comfort Bedding
                  Peak Industrial Estate
                       Newtown
                      Lancashire
                       LA5 9OP

                  Tel 01567 123456
                  Fax 01567 123457
              sales@comfort-bedding.co.uk
              www.comfort-bedding.co.uk

                 VAT Reg 345 7892 00
```

Invoice no. 125889   Tax point date: 19/02/01

To:

Majestic Hotel
Main Road
Brighton
East Sussex
BN1 3AB

Your order no. *5654*				Delivery note no. *19873*		
Ref. no.	**Quantity**	**Description**	**Unit value £**	**Total**	**VAT @ 17.5%**	**Total**
123456	25	135 × 190 cm divan beds	185.00	4625.00	809.38	5434.38
			Totals	4625.00	809.38	5434.38
				Amount due:		5434.38

Payment terms strictly 28 days

E & OE

Figure 6.6 *Invoice*

authorized. The accounts department in the buying organization will then record the amount owed and the name of the creditor in the purchase ledger and record the value of the goods bought in the purchaser's account.

If the order form, goods received note and invoice differ, the accounts department will usually ask the supplier to amend the invoice. This is done by means of credit and debit notes.

Debit and credit notes

If the buyer has been asked to pay too much, the seller will issue a credit note for the difference. The amount on the credit note will be entered by the accounts department into the buyer's account in the purchase ledger. This will reduce the amount owed by the buyer to the organization.

If the buyer has been asked to pay too little, the seller issues a debit note for the difference; the amount is then entered into the buyer's account in the purchase ledger. This will increase the amount owed by the buyer to the organization.

Statement of account

When a customer buys from a supplier on a regular basis using credit, payment will be made on receipt of a monthly statement of account from the supplier. Payments made in this way avoid the need to send a cheque for every invoice when it falls due, thereby reducing administration costs and bank charges. It also acts as a way of delaying payment, since a purchase of goods which may be made at the start of the month will not appear on the statement until the following month.

The statement of account will list:

- **the amount brought forward from the previous statement**
- **purchases made during the month**
- **payments made since the last statement**
- **the total amount due to be paid**
- **the balance outstanding**

Pay slip

Providing the invoice has been approved as correct, the accounts department will request authorization for payment from the purchasing department. This is done in the form of a pay slip.

The pay slip is a security measure used by organizations to ensure that no payments are made before the goods are checked. It takes the form of a simple document which is signed by an authorized person who instructs the accounts department to pay for the goods or services purchased. The pay slip could be in the form of:

- **a document which gives details of the goods bought and includes room for the signature of an authorized person**
- **a rubber stamp which is placed on a copy of the invoice and sent to the authorized person for signing**

- **a space on the delivery note allowing a signature for authorizing payment (see Figure 6.5 on page 224).**

The important detail is that it must be signed by a person with authority before payment is made.

Security measures and consequences

It is very important for an organization to have built-in security measures. This will help to minimize the following:

- **pilfering, for example goods being bought for personal use or taken from stores for personal use**
- **wasted expenditure – goods being bought that are not really necessary**
- **errors in the production of invoices and cheques**
- **paying for goods or services that are damaged or are not received at all**
- **unauthorized employees writing cheques for goods**
- **fraud when payment is made by cash**

The security measures used have been discussed in this chapter and are summarized in Figure 6.7.

Petty cash voucher system

Some goods and services need to be purchased using cash, usually because they are of such a small value or are needed urgently from a local supplier. For example, employees may be asked to buy some bread rolls, or they may have had to use their own money on travelling expenses for the benefit of the organization. In these situations, employees will need to obtain the cash prior to the purchase or be reimbursed at a later date.

A control procedure needs to be in place for these types of purchase for auditing and VAT purposes and to minimize the temptation of the light fingered. The procedure generally used is the petty cash voucher system. Here, a clerk will have the responsibility for issuing or reimbursing cash to employees. The employee will be asked to complete a petty cash voucher and have it signed by an authorized person (see Figure 6.8). On completion of the voucher, the cash will be issued and recorded in the petty cash book.

It is important that the person who is purchasing or has purchased the goods gives a receipt to the clerk for auditing and VAT purposes. This is called a strict receipt system.

Stage	Buyer	Seller
Order	Issue only with authorized signature	Check for credit worthiness
Delivery note	Stores: check goods are not damaged and quantity matches delivery note. If OK, issue a goods received note in triplicate.	Ensure it is signed by buyer on delivery
Goods received note	Stores: keep one copy as record of goods received into stores Purchasing: match goods received note with the original order	
Invoice	Accounts: check invoice against original order, delivery note and goods received note – if they do not match, contact seller to rectify; if they match, request pay slip from purchasing	On receipt of signed delivery note, make out invoice, have it checked by someone else before posting
Overcharged on invoice	Ask for credit note, enter into purchase ledger to reduce amount due	Issue a credit note, enter into sales ledger to decrease amount due
Undercharged on invoice		Issue a debit note, enter into sales ledger to increase amount due
Pay slip	Purchasing: if all four agree, authorize payment; only an authorized person should sign	

Figure 6.7 *Security measures*

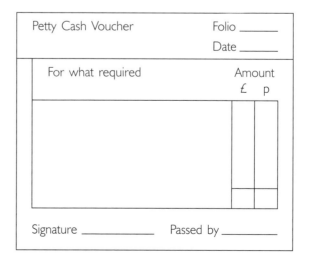

Figure 6.8 *Petty cash voucher*

Calculating the selling price

Every type of outlet needs to determine the cost of products and services provided in order to assess whether or not they are operating effectively and to enable them to calculate appropriate selling prices.

Much of the basic information required to determine costs originates from records maintained at the various stages of the process of purchasing, receiving, storage and issuing. In addition, the selling price is usually arrived at by a study of the demand for the product. Managers within the industry need to ensure that the amount received in sales income (revenue) covers the cost of providing the services and facilities. They also need to control the costs so that the company/outlet can be more competitive and profitable.

To do this, it is important to understand how costs behave and the ways in which the overheads are spread across the whole operation.

Types of costs

Direct costs

Sometimes called variable costs or prime costs, direct costs fluctuate with the level of activity. Examples include:

- **material costs (food, drink)**
- **fuel**
- **packaging**
- **wages of direct labour**

For example, in a hotel, in which the à la carte restaurant has on its menu Beef Wellington, the following direct costs will be incurred:

- **direct materials – raw materials, i.e. the ingredients needed to produce the dish**
- **direct labour – the wages of the chef, waiter, etc., plus staff meals, staff uniforms, etc.**
- **power – electricity and gas to cook the dish**

Indirect costs

Indirect costs (sometimes called overheads or fixed costs) are all the remaining costs of a business. These costs do not fluctuate with the level of activity. They will comprise a large section of the initial set-up costs of a new business or new activity. Examples of fixed costs are:

- ✪ **Rent, rates and interest on loans**
- ✪ **Insurance**
- ✪ **Heating**

In the hotel used in the example above, these indirect costs may be incurred:

- ✪ **management salaries**
- ✪ **administration staffing and stationery**
- ✪ **reception department**
- ✪ **marketing costs including salaries**
- ✪ **running expenses**
- ✪ **rent, rates, heat and light, maintenance**
- ✪ **depreciation (see below)**

Depreciation

Consider your family car or your own car. Do you think it could be resold for the same amount as it cost to buy? The answer is no (unless it is a very unusual model or a collector's or classic car). This is because the wear and tear on the car has increased. The reduction in value caused by wear and tear is called depreciation.

Computers and computer software depreciate more quickly as they become technically out of date. The term used for this is obsolescence. It is the same for all businesses. Most fixed assets bought for use within the business will lose value over time – the older they become or the more they are used, the less is the resale value. Equipment such as cookers, freezers, bedroom and restaurant furniture will lose value and the reduction in value (depreciation) is therefore an indirect cost to the organization.

Strictly speaking some production costs do not fit neatly into either indirect or direct. This is because they comprise both a fixed element and a variable element. A good example would be telephone costs where there is a fixed charge for rental plus a variable charge for usage. Other examples include electricity, gas and overtime for fixed salary workers. These costs are known as semi-variable costs.

Units of goods and services

In the hospitality and catering industry many goods and services are provided. In simple terms, each product or service can be identified as a unit, either on its own or as part of a group of related products and services. Examples of a unit include a dish, a menu, a bedroom, a function. The types of cost which make up a dish are quite easy to identify. When calculating the cost of roast beef, direct costs would include:

- ✪ **ingredients**
- ✪ **the chef's wages**
- ✪ **the waiter's/waitress's wages**
- ✪ **electricity/gas used**

And indirect costs would include:

- ✪ **rent, rates, heat, light**
- ✪ **marketing costs**
- ✪ **administration costs**
- ✪ **management salaries**
- ✪ **depreciation of the equipment**

When providing a bedroom direct costs would include:

- ✪ **laundry**
- ✪ **soaps and cleaning materials**
- ✪ **room assistant's wages**
- ✪ **electricity/gas used**

And indirect costs would include:

- ✪ **rent, rates, general heat and light**
- ✪ **marketing**
- ✪ **reception**
- ✪ **administration**
- ✪ **maintenance**
- ✪ **management salaries**
- ✪ **depreciation of furniture**
- ✪ **depreciation of cleaning equipment**

How the selling price is calculated

Whatever is being sold, the method for calculating the selling price is the same. The formula to remember is:

COST + PROFIT = SELLING PRICE

The selling price always represents 100%.

Example

Find the selling price of a beefburger to achieve a gross profit percentage (or kitchen percentage) of 80% on the selling price if the food cost is 42p.

COST + PROFIT = SELLING PRICE

Profit of 80% means that the cost price represents 20% (100% − 80%)

$\dfrac{\text{Cost price}}{20}$ represents 1%

$\dfrac{\text{Cost price}}{20} \times 100$ represents 100%

So selling price $= \dfrac{42p}{20} \times \dfrac{100}{1} = £2.10$

We find 1% of the cost by dividing the absolute food cost (42p) by its percentage of the selling price (20%). We then multiply this figure by 100 to find the value equivalent to 100%, i.e. the selling price.

Activity 6.1

Ray Self, the Catering Manager in a university hall of residence, has noticed that the average gross profit (or kitchen percentage) is 25%. At a recent meeting of all Catering Managers at the university, it was decided that an average gross profit of 35% must be achieved.

What can Ray do to increase the gross profit percentage?

Wastage

Excessive wastage in a kitchen can result from:

- **poor purchasing**
- **poor culinary skills**
- **poor storage controls**

Some wastage occurs naturally during preparation and this must be taken into account when ordering food from a supplier.

Example

If a chef wants to serve 75 × 125 g portions of minced beef and he estimates 15% of the meat will be wasted through cooking, how much should he order?

Method:

Amount of meat to be ordered	= 100% (A)
Amount wasted	= 15% (B)
∴ Meat to be served (A–B)	= 85%
Meat to be served	= 75 × 125 g = 9.375 kg
	= 85% of order

$$\frac{9.375}{85} \times \frac{100}{1} = 11.029 \text{ kg to order}$$

We find 1% of the meat to be served by dividing the total meat to be served (9.375 kg) by the percentage of meat to be served (85%) after allowing for wastage. We multiply this figure by 100 to get the total weight of meat which needs to be ordered. In most cases the amount is rounded up to the nearest 500 g or kilo, so in this instance it is likely that 11.5 kg will be ordered. If 11 kg is ordered and wastage is slightly more than 15%, the yield will not be high enough to satisfy the need for 75 portions.

Apportionment of costs

Costs that are not specific to the production of a product are apportioned (shared) across each of the establishment departments, for example reception, management.

Overheads can be apportioned in many different ways. For example, the unallocated repairs and maintenance may be apportioned to departments on the basis of turnover. Other bases of apportionment may involve departmental floor space, for example square metres or cubic metres, or they may involve departmental wages.

While different organizations choose different methods, the main point to remember is that the method chosen to apportion costs must be fair. Whichever method is chosen, the following procedure is adopted:

1   **Find the total cost of the overhead to be apportioned**
2   **Find the total units involved in the method chosen, for example the total meals, bedrooms sold, employee wages, etc. – the units selected will then be added together across departments**
3   **Divide the total cost by the total units (of chosen method) to get an overhead cost per unit**
4   **Multiply the overhead cost per unit by the total units in each department to get an overhead cost per department**

Pricing considerations

Managers have to determine an initial set of prices, for example when devising a menu. Managers also have to revise existing prices in order to recover cost increases, to increase the volume of sales, to counteract the competition or to reflect changes in the national budget such as a higher tax on alcoholic drinks.

There are three main methods of calculating the initial price:

1   **Cost plus an appropriate margin to give a predetermined gross profit percentage. This can be done by using the same percentage on every dish (for example 60%) or the same percentage can be applied to a group of dishes (for example starters 80%, vegetables 85%, etc.). In non-profit catering businesses the amount added on may be negligible, so that dishes are sold at cost price.**

2   **Ratio of price to cost can also determine prices, e.g. starters might be 4 : 1, main courses 2 : 1, etc.**

3   **Adding a fixed amount of money (for example 50p) to the portion cost of each dish, or differing amounts to each group of dishes.**

Some establishments will use pricing methods based on managerial judgement and local market conditions. In practice, this means charging what managers feel the market can bear, pricing at or below competitors' prices or following the price of the market leader.

Commercial catering organizations often offer discounts, generally to attract a new segment of the market.

Non-commercial catering organizations (for example work canteens) are often subsidized by the company which they are serving. This results in staff being able to purchase meals at a reduced cost, with the company making up the difference.

Some restaurants and hotels still make an additional charge for service and this is shown separately on the bill. The service charge is added before the calculation for VAT is made (see Figure 6.9, page 236). The service charge should be distributed among the staff.

Value Added Tax

Organizations that are registered for Value Added Tax (VAT) must produce bills, invoices and receipts that include the VAT registration number, the date of sale and the rate of VAT charged (currently 17.5%).

	£
Food and drink	49.50
Service charge (10%)	4.95
Sub-total	54.45
VAT (17.5%)	9.53
Total	63.98

Figure 6.9 *Customer's restaurant bill*

Nearly every time you make a purchase you will receive a sales receipt. The next time you buy something keep your receipt and identify:

- ✪ **VAT registration number**
- ✪ **the date the sale was made**
- ✪ **the amount of the sale**
- ✪ **the amount of the sale excluding VAT**

Calculating VAT

Sometimes a receipt will state the amount of the sale and then add on the VAT to arrive at the total sale. But at other times the receipt will include the amount of VAT. When recording financial transactions it is important to be able to identify the amount of VAT charged so that it can be recorded separately in the accounts of the organization.

Assuming a VAT rate of 17.5%, the example below illustrates the calculations of VAT due on a sale of £100.00:

Sale £100.00

$$\text{VAT at } 17.5\% = \frac{100.00 \times 17.5}{100} \qquad £17.50$$

Total sale £117.50

But if the amount included VAT at 17.5%, the calculation would be:

Sale (including VAT at 17.5%) £117.50

$$\text{VAT charged} = \frac{117.50 \times 17.5}{117.5} \qquad £17.50$$

Sale (excluding VAT) £100.00

VAT is chargeable on all products and services, except for visitors paid out (VPO) or disbursements (for example theatre tickets or taxi fares paid for by the hotel on behalf of the guest) and newspapers.

If a guest's stay in an hotel exceeds four weeks, VAT is only chargeable for meals, extras and on that part of the charge for accommodation which represents the provision of 'facilities' other than the right to occupy the room. The provision of facilities is to be taken as not less than 20 per cent of the amount payable for the accommodation and facilities.

Ways of controlling costs

Standard recipes

Standard recipes are designed to ensure dish quality and to control costs. A standard recipe provides details of ingredients and cooking methods in order to ensure a consistent, accurately costed end-product.

Standard menus

Standard menus also provide a means of controlling costs and assisting in purchasing requirements. Many organizations now have standard menus which are designed to ensure that a range of complimentary dishes is offered and that the menu is nutritionally balanced.

The à la carte menu has developed into the standard menus favoured by hotel companies such as Forte who have the same menus in all their branded restaurants. Also, restaurants like Little Chef, Pizza Express and Pizza Hut all have standard menus. These menus reflect the corporate image and customers know what to expect. Managers also know precisely how much profit they are making.

Further information on types of menus can be found in Unit 2.

Yield Testing

One method of examining potential cost savings, particularly in food preparation, is by yield testing. This is a way of checking to see that waste during the preparation and cooking stages is kept within acceptable limits; from this is taken the yield specification.

For example, suppose a hospital kitchen is producing large quantities of apple crumble. Rather than use a standard recipe, it could purchase different brands of A10 solid-pack apple and ready-prepared crumble mix. Then, over a period of time, a decision would be reached on which brand to use based on the quality of each product and the yield it produced. The opinion of the manager and chef and customer reactions would be taken into account.

The results of yield testing can be easily kept on simple record cards or on a computerized database.

Storage and issuing

Stock control

Stock control (holding stocks) costs money and therefore many organizations use computers to determine the optimum stock level. It is essential that organizations have a good stock control system, the objective being to strike a balance between having too few stocks and holding too many stocks – both have disadvantages. Figure 6.10 shows a stock record card used in some establishments.

A good stock control system will provide:

✪ **control over the movement of stock in and out of the stores**

✪ **control over the level of stock**

✪ **stock records from which information can easily be taken regarding orders placed, goods received and issues made from the stores**

Most organizations will employ a storekeeper. This is a very responsible position. Depending on the establishment, the storekeeper may be responsible for:

STOCK RECORD CARD									
BIN No. *73*							SUPPLIER *BOOKERS*		
COMMODITY *Evaporated milk*									
RE-ORDER QUANTITY: 3 × 24 (72)									
Date	Ref.	Unit cost	Received		Issued		Balance	
			No.	£	No.	£	No.	£
1/10/01	1279	24p	144	34.56			144	34.56
2/10/01	0013	24p			10	2.40	134	32.16
4/10/01	0056	24p			24	5.76	110	26.40
5/10/01	1311	24p	72	17.28			182	43.68

Figure 6.10 *Stock record card*

- ○ ordering
- ○ receiving
- ○ storing all goods
- ○ issuing
- ○ keeping records
- ○ stock security

Storage

All goods that are purchased will have to be stored within the organization upon delivery. Where the goods will be stored, under what conditions and for what period of time will vary according to the type of product. All goods will have to be stored in a secure area which is designated for the storage of that particular type of commodity.

Beds, mattresses, bed boards and cots will normally be stored in an area which allows easy access to the bedrooms and is dry and cool.

Frozen foodstuffs will of course need to be stored in freezers in a part of the food store. Food stores are generally located near to the kitchens but away from any heat sources. Store rooms usually face north (to avoid being heated by the sun).

Liquor is stored in a cellar which is kept at an ambient temperature and humidity level. The cellar is generally located within easy reach of the bar and the delivery point to enable easy transportation of heavy barrels, etc.

Dry food goods are stored off the floor on racking in a cool store room.

Hazardous chemicals must be stored under appropriate conditions and in suitable locations and their access must be tightly controlled. You can find more information on this in Unit 5.

Documents used in stock control

Bin cards

A separate bin card is originated for each commodity and records the quantities of goods received into and issued from the stores (see Figure 6.11).

Regular spot checks should be made on the goods held in stock; this means that a few items daily should be physically counted and checked against the balance on the bin card. This spot checking should be planned so that all major items have been checked at least once during an accounting period, usually every six months or once a year. In addition to spot checks, food and beverage controllers should make surprise stock checks and no prior notice should be given to the storekeeper or his/her staff on these occasions. Any discrepancies noted should be notified immediately to the management and corrective action taken.

BIN CARD				
COMMODITY: Evaporated Milk		RE-ORDER: 3 × 24		
MINIMUM STOCK: 6 × 24 (144)		SUPPLIER: Bookers		
MAXIMUM STOCK: 12 × 24 (288)				
Date	**Ref.**	**Received**	**Issued**	**Balance**
01/10/01	1279	144	–	144
02/10/01	0013	–	10	134
04/10/01	0056	–	24	110
05/10/01	1311	72	–	182

Figure 6.11 *Bin card*

Stock list								
Bin number	**Description of item**	**Unit**	**Quantity**	**Unit price**	**Total value**	**When last checked**	**Discrepancy**	**Remarks**
1	Apple puree	kg	1	1.95	1.95	01/02/01		
2	Apple segments	500 g	2	1.00	2.00	01/02/01		
3	Almond essence	150 ml	3	3.50	10.50	01/02/01		

Figure 6.12 *Stock list*

Stock record card

The stock record card shows the monetary value of goods booked into and out of the stores (see Figure 6.10, page 238).

Stock lists

Stocktaking should be done at least once a month. Stock sheets listing all commodities held in stock are usually printed, so that it is a simple procedure to fill in the balance of each commodity at a certain date. From the stock sheets, the total capital invested in stock can be ascertained, as well as the rate of turnover of stock and stock levels of all commodities. Details on the stock lists (see Figure 6.12) are:

1   bin number

2   item

3   unit in which stocked

4   quantity – number of units in stock

5   unit price

6   total value of stock – quantity × unit price

7   date of last stock check

8   discrepancy (if any) between figure in quantity column and that on stock record card

9   any remarks regarding state of stock such as damage, deterioration, etc.

Presentation and use of data and information

Data and information must be presented clearly and must be easily understood by those using and needing the information. The presenter of the information must know where the information has come from, how it was prepared and what it relates to. You will need to learn how to present numerical information in a format which is accepted by the industry and is appropriate to the user.

Customer bills and accounts

How a bill and/or account is presented to a customer will depend on the outlet. In a fast food outlet, like for example McDonald's, bills are not given to customers. In some cafes and restaurants, customers are given a handwritten bill which details the food and drink which has been supplied, the costs for each item and the total amount due. Other restaurants will produce computer printed bills which show the details of the food and drink ordered, the date, name of the person serving the table, number of covers, food service charge, etc.

In hotels, either handwritten or computer printed bills are used which show details of the customer's name, room occupied, dates, services provided, extras, room rate, etc. (see Figure 6.13).

Forecasting

Forecasting the level of future business in numerical and financial terms requires experience of the industry and the establishment and a knowledge of the past trading history as well as a knowledge of anticipated events. By looking at past turnover figures and other statistical information, it is possible to identify trends in occupancy levels and covers served. There are several times throughout the year when busy periods can be anticipated, for example New Year, Valentine's Day, Easter, Mothering Sunday, Father's Day, Christmas. In areas around universities, restaurants are often busy at graduation. At regional and national sporting events, establishments in the surrounding areas will be able to predict peaks, for example Ascot, Henley Regatta, Newmarket Races, Wimbledon.

In order to be able to calculate occupancy levels, you need to know the maximum occupancy and the actual or predicted occupancy levels. For example, in a hotel with 125 twin bedded rooms, 50 double bedded

King's Road, Brighton, East Sussex, BN1 2FW   Telephone: **01273 321188**   Fax: 01273 202694

DE VERE HOTELS

MS D BROWN
12 BEECH WAY
OLDTOWN
OT1 2AB

Folio No.	479929	Room No.	123	Arrival:	19/06/99	Departure:	20/06/99

	Date	Description	Amount
1	19/06/99	CAR PARKING.........	11.00
2	19/06/99	ACCOMMODATION.......	110.00
3	20/06/99	VISA/ACCESS.........	121.00CR

EXAMPLE

```
:        V A T   A N A L Y S I S           : INVOICE    ┌──────────┐
: VAT EXCLUSIVE VAT RATE VAT AMOUNT VAT INCLUSIVE :  TOTAL     │    .00   │
:        102.98  17.50 %    18.02      121.00    :           └──────────┘
:                                                :
:                                                : VAT VALUE
:                                                : INCLUDED IN ┌──────────┐
:                                                : THIS INVOICE│  18.02   │
:                                                :           └──────────┘
:        102.98             18.02      121.00    :
: -------------          ---------- -------------:
*----------------------------------------------------------*
      Visitors should receive an official receipt for all payments made.        Signature _____

      VAT Reg. No. 151 6512 88
```

De Vere Hotels is a division of Greenalls Hotels & Leisure Limited.
Registered in England: Registration Number 418878. Registered Office: Wilderspool House, Warrington WA4 6RH.
A member of the Greenalls Group Plc.

Figure 6.13   *Computer printed hotel bill*
Courtesy of The Grand Hotel, Brighton

rooms and 25 singles, the maximum number of rooms that could be let in the month of June is 6000 (125 + 50 + 25 × 30 days). The maximum number of sleepers (not allowing for extra beds or cots and assuming that each twin or double room accommodated two people) would be 11250 (250 + 100 + 25 × 30 days).

Using the above figures, if during the month of June a total of 4500 bedrooms were let, the room occupancy percentage would be 75% (4500 divided by 6000).

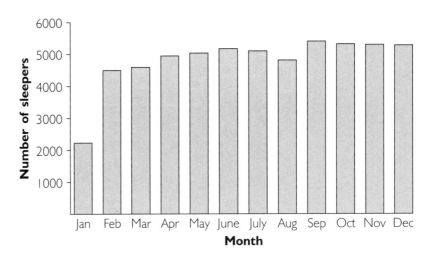

Figure 6.14 *Sleeper occupancy figures*

Sleeper occupancy figures can be presented in a graph, as shown in Figure 6.14.

It is possible to find out the total number of covers served per session and also the total amount spent on food and drink. In order to calculate the average spend, you need to divide the total spend by the number of customers. For example:

Total spent on food	£985.00
Total spent on drink	£156.85
Total	£1141.85

Total number of covers 50

Average spend (£1141.85 ÷ 50) = £22.84 (to the nearest penny)

It is essential to be able to calculate the actual occupancy levels and covers served in order to ensure that the costings are still accurate and that profit levels are being achieved, in addition to providing an information source for the marketing department.

It is also necessary to be able to predict accurately the occupancy levels and covers served in order that resources can be obtained (staffing as well as laundry, food and drink) and managed – managers do not want to employ staff unnecessarily and do not want to hold surplus stocks of food and drink. Conversely, managers do want to be prepared and to have sufficient numbers of staff on duty and sufficient food and drink available.

The number of covers served can be presented in a graph, as shown in Figure 6.15. Identifying the peaks and troughs of the business will also assist when planning maintenance and staff training.

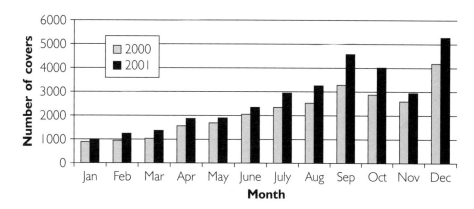

Figure 6.15 *Covers served by room service, 2000 and 2001*

Summaries of sales and costs

The area in the establishment which deals with the processing of customers' transactions will be able to present a breakdown of the day's takings into different departments within the organization. Depending on the system used, it may also be able to identify the number of portions of a certain dish sold, the number of measures of spirits sold, etc. as well as the total of sales handled by different members of staff.

Profit and loss accounts and trading statements

At the end of an accounting period (usually a year) a profit and loss account and a trading statement should be produced so that the financial position of the organization is clear. It is of course possible to generate these statements at more frequent intervals and shorter versions may be used on a weekly or monthly basis so that managers have a clear idea of the financial state of the business.

Revision questions

1   Mark each of the following statements true (T) or false (F):

(a)   The cost of raw materials used in making a product is a direct cost

(b)   Direct costs include the salaries of marketing personnel   (2 marks)

2   The following is a list of receipts received by Fast Service Ltd for items bought out of petty cash. They all include a VAT charge of 17.5%. Calculate the amount of (i) VAT and (ii) the sale price exclusive of VAT, both to the nearest pence.

(a) £20.00
(b) £13.50
(c) £86.75
(d) £3.78
(e) £54.75   (10 marks)

3 The following indicators can be used to evaluate performance:

A   Average spend
B   Stock turnover
C   Gross profit
D   Net profit

Which indicator best matches the following descriptions?

(a) Sales less the cost of purchases
(b) Total sales divided by average stock
(c) Total sales divided by the number of customers   (6 marks)

4 A steak house franchise uses a centralized buying system but some items are still bought-in as cash purchases. Which of the following is likely to be the most frequent cash purchase:

(a) Fresh flowers
(b) Dishwasher powder
(c) Frozen peas
(d) Paper serviettes   (2 marks)

5 The assistant manager of a nursing home telephones a vegetable order to a supplier. The delivery arrives but some items are unfit so they are sent back with the driver. Which is the correct sequence for the paperwork involved?

(a) Credit note – invoice – delivery note – receipt
(b) Delivery note – invoice – receipt – credit note

(c) Delivery note – receipt – credit note – invoice
(d) Delivery note – credit note – invoice – receipt   (2 marks)

6 For effective purchasing, purchase specifications are used for some items. A private hospital caterer is most likely to draw up a purchase specification for:

(a) Postage stamps for office paperwork
(b) Exotic vegetables for a directors' meal
(c) Fresh flowers for a visitors' reception
(d) Patients' meal trays to be used on all wards   (2 marks)

7 The following are documents used in stock control:

A   Stores requisition
B   Bin card
C   Stocktaking records
D   Stock list

Which document shows:

(a) The theoretical total of stock held?
(b) The actual level of stock?
(c) An entry for each movement of stock?   (6 marks)

8 A hotel has calculated the price for a proposed company function and told the customer the cost. The customer insists on a lower price without any change to the package. What must be reduced if the hotel wants the business?

(a) Overheads
(b) Profit
(c) Direct costs
(d) Indirect costs   (2 marks)

Unit 6 key skills

Keys to attainment

These are key skills or aspects of key skills that are central to the Purchasing, Costing and Control unit. The key to attainment shows that the relevant aspect of the key skill has also been achieved. You will of course need to develop and practise the key skill during your lessons and in your private studies.

Application of number, level 3

When you are:	You should have achieved the following key skills evidence:
Planning how to collect information for calculating costs and prices of simple and complex products and services	N3.1 Plan and interpret information from two different types of sources, including a large data set.
Using formulae and calculating costs and prices for simple and complex products and services	N3.2 Carry out multi-stage calculations to do with: A amounts and sizes B scales and proportion C rearranging and using formulae
Presenting at least two results of calculated data, such as showing how the categories of costs relate to sales and prices.	N3.3 Interpret results of calculations, present findings and justify methods. Use at least one graph, one chart and one diagram.

Communication, level 3

When you are:	You should have achieved the following key skills evidence:
Finding information about the cost and price of goods and discounts or special offers available	C3.2 Read and synthesize information from two extended documents about a complex subject. One of these documents should include at least one image.
Preparing a set of purchasing cycle documents Preparing information about monitoring and controlling costs and sales	C3.3 Write two different types of documents about complex subjects. One piece of writing should be an extended document and include at least one image.

Signposts

These are naturally occurring opportunities for the development of key skills through your learning and assessment. You will not necessarily achieve the signposted key skill through your evidence for the Purchasing, Costing and Control unit. You will need to develop additional evidence elsewhere to ensure that you meet the requirements of the key skills units fully.

Communication, level 3

If you are:	There may be opportunities for you to develop the following key skills evidence:
Participating in a discussion about monitoring and controlling costs and sales	C3.1b Make a presentation about a complex subject, using at least one image to illustrate complex points.
Presenting results of data you have collected or calculated	C3.2 Read and synthesize information from two extended documents about a complex subject. One of these documents should include at least one image.

Information Technology, level 3

If you are:	There may be opportunities for you to develop the following key skills evidence:
Finding information about the cost and price of goods and discounts or special offers available	IT 3.1 Plan and use different sources to search for and select information required for two different purposes.
Preparing a set of purchasing cycle documents Calculating costs and prices for simple and complex products and services	IT 3.2 Explore, develop and exchange information and derive new information to meet two different purposes.
Preparing a set of purchasing cycle documents Preparing information about monitoring and controlling costs and sales	IT 3.3 Present information from different sources for two different purposes and audiences. Include at least one example of text, one example of images and one example of numbers.

Unit no.	Key skills reference								
	N3.1	**N3.2**	**N3.3**	**C3.1**	**C3.2**	**C3.3**	**IT 3.1**	**IT 3.2**	**IT 3.3**
1	●	●	●	◊			◊	◊	◊
2				◊	●	●		◊	◊
3				◊ ●	●	●	◊	◊	◊
4				◊ ●	●	●	◊	◊	◊
5	◊	◊	◊	●	●	●	◊	◊	◊
6	●	●	●	◊	◊ ●	●	◊	◊	◊

◊ Signpost ● Key to attainment

Key skills signposting and attainment grid

Appendix: Drink compendium

Beers, cider, etc.

Item	Description	Example
BEER	Alcoholic beverage from fermentation of cereals	
Ingredients		
Liquor	Water minerally suitable for beer	Newcastle Brown
Malt	From barley (Maltose)	light/dark
Hops	Bitter, lupalin	Fuggles, Goldings
Sugar	Invert for fermentation, caramel for colour	
Yeast	Brewers	Saccharomyces cervisiae/carlsbergensis
Production		
Malting	Conversion of starch to sugar – grist	Diastase
Mashing	In mash tun to make flavoured wort	
Brewing	Boiling in copper with sugar and hops	Flavour
Fermentation	Top with cervisiae for ales Bottom carlbergensis for lagers	
Clarifying	Filter (hopback) cook, rack	
Conditioning	Traditional: Racking, priming, dry hopping Modern: Chill, filter, centrifuge, pasteurize, carbonate	Barrel Finish off

Styles		
Lager	Bottom fermented and cold stored	Carlsberg
Mild	Usually dark, less hops and alcohol, draught	
Brown	Dark, less hops, bottle	Newcastle
Pale & light	Pale, bottled	Burton
Bitter	Pale, more hops, draught	
Stout	Dark, soft	Guinness
Strong	Higher in alcohol – 4–11%	
Barley wines	Fuller flavoured alcoholic	
Low alcohol	Less than 1.2%, vacuum distillation or reverse osmosis	
Non-alcoholic	Less than 0.5%, vacuum distillation or reverse osmosis	

Item	Description	Example
Measures	1/2 pint, bottles 1/3, 1/2 (275 mls)	
Bottles	1/3, 1/2 pint (275 mls)	
Barrels		
Pin	4.5 gal (approx 4.5 litres to a gallon)	
Firkin	9 gal	
Kilderkin	18 gal	
Barrel	36 gal (now often 100 litres)	
Hogshead	54 gal	
Butt	108 gal	
CIDER	Fermented apple juice, 1.2–8.5% alcohol Bottled, pasteurised, filtered, carbonated	Draught scrumpy, cloudy
PERRY	Fermented pear juice	Babycham
SAKE	Rice beer (18% alcohol)	

Cocktails – Mixed drinks of three or more ingredients

Equipment   Stirring glass, bar spoon, hawthorn strainer (jug with spoon),
             cocktail shaker, electric blender, liquidiser
             Glasses: 3 oz cocktail glass tumblers – old fashioned, Slim Jim, etc.

Ingredients Spirits: gin, whisky, vodka, rum, brandy, tequila, etc.
             Liqueurs: Cointreau, etc.
             Liqueur wines: vermouths, etc.
             Fresh fruit, juices, egg, cream, etc.
             Grenadine, gomme syrup, Angostura, orange bitters

Decoration   Lemon slices and twists, cherries, onions, olives, fruit, parasols, etc.

Preparation methods

Stirred   Spirits, liqueurs and/or liqueur wines: ice in stirring glass, quickly stir, strain with
             hawthorn strainer usually into cocktail glass

Dry Martini	2 parts gin to 1 (or less) part dry vermouth, twist of lemon
Sweet Martini	2 parts gin to 1 part sweet Martini, cherry
Manhattan	2 parts whisky to 1 part sweet vermouth, dash of Angostura, cherry

Shaken   Ingredients as for stirred + fruit juice, cream or egg yolks/white, cocktail glass
             Ice in shaker + ingredients, lid firmly on, shake hard at shoulder height, strain through
             lid

White Lady	2 parts gin + 1 part Cointreau + 1 part fresh lemon juice, optional egg white
Sidecar	2 parts brandy + 1 part Cointreau + 1 part fresh lemon juice
Daiquiri	3 parts white rum + 1 part fresh lime juice, gomme syrup, optional egg white
Sours	2 parts named spirit + 1 part fresh lemon juice + gomme syrup

Build   Ingredients into tall glass without premixing

Tequila sunrise	Orange juice, tequila + dash of grenadine

Blend   All ingredients with fruit, ice cream, eggs etc., crushed or shaved ice all in, blast, not strained

Pina colada	2 parts pineapple juice + 1 part white rum + 1 part coconut cream

Longer

Collins	2 named spirits, 1 fresh lemon juice + gomme in Slim Jim filled with ice. Top up with soda
Pimms	Gin-based product + lemonade in 250 ml glass, orange, lemon, cucumber, borage or mint leaf

Hot

Toddy	Spirit + sugar + boiling water – slice lemon + nutmeg

	Irish coffee	2 spoons sugar + coffee, stir, add Irish whisky, float double cream using teaspoon
Digestif	*Brandy Alexander*	1 brandy + 1 creme de cacao + 2 double cream, shake
Champagne	*Cocktail*	Angostura dripped on sugar lump in saucer, glass with dash of brandy, top up with champagne
	Bucks Fizz	1 part orange juice + 2 parts champagne in a flute
Non-alcoholic	*Pussyfoot*	Orange + lemon + lime juices, egg yolk and grenadine, shaker or blend
Pousse cafe	Liqueurs and spirits stacked in a liqueur glass – no mix – dependent on density	
	Rainbow	Creme de cacao, violette, yellow chartreuse, maraschino, Benedictine, brandy
	Traffic light	Creme de menthe, advocaat, cherry brandy
Correctif or Pick-me-ups	*Prairie Oyster*	Whole egg yolk, Worcestershire and tomato sauce, vinegar and black pepper

Wine

Wine is the alcoholic drink made from grapes. Wine is made for enjoyment, so allow it to enhance meals and social occasions.

It can vary a great deal – find the style you like and which suits the situation.

Wines can vary in colour, sweetness and weight as well as flavour, quality and production.

Some wines are better with food, others without.

Take advice, but do experiment and have fun.

Glasses

All wines should be drunk in glasses large enough to give the wine room to breathe, probably 200 ml and only just over half full (6 glasses from a bottle). When drinking quality wines a stemmed glass is preferable.

Service

Ideally buy wine in advance. Wine should be stored horizontally in a cool dark place.

White, rose, sparkling and light reds taste better if lightly chilled.

Fuller reds are better if allowed to gently acquire 16–18°C.

Cut the foil and then open with a good corkscrew (Screwpull highly recommended).

Main wine styles

- ✪ **Dry sparkling (brut)**   Champagne, Saumur – at celebrations, as an aperitif
- ✪ **Dry liqueur wines**   Fino sherry, dry vermouth – as an aperitif, with hors d'oeuvres
- ✪ **Dry light white**   Chablis, Muscadet – with seafood, particularly shellfish
- ✪ **Dry fruity white**   Alsace, Riesling, Sauvignon – with fish, lighter meats, chicken
- ✪ **Dry fuller white**   Burgundy, Chardonnay, Soave – with fish and light meats
- ✪ **Medium dry white**   Germany, Riesling, Saumur – any time with fish, starters
- ✪ **Light fruity red**   Beaujolais, Gamay, Vin de Pays – any time for a picnic, lunch
- ✪ **Medium bodied red**   Claret, Cabernet Sauvignon, Chianti – with lamb, pork, turkey
- ✪ **Fuller bodied red**   Burgundy, Pinot Noir, Rhone – with beef and other meats
- ✪ **Full bodied red**   Châteauneuf-du-Pape, Barolo, Rioja, Dao – with game, full cheeses
- ✪ **Sweet white**   Sauternes, Auslese, Muscat – with dessert, sweet dishes, also pâté
- ✪ **Sweet liqueur wines**   Port, Madeira, Muscat – with dessert, cheese, after meals
- ✪ **Sweet sparkling**   Rich, Demi-sec, Asti Spumante – with dessert or any time

These are only suggestions. There are no rules except: **try, if you like it, that's fine**.

If you are having more than one wine, young before old, dry before sweet are usually sensible but not essential.

Any wine left can be kept if refrigerated with minimum air (vacuum) or in as small a bottle as possible. The lighter wines will only keep a day but some fuller, very sweet wines will keep for a week or more.

All leftovers are great in cooking and can add a lovely flavour to the simplest dish.

Tasting and evaluation of wine

Look Smell Taste – spit Record	Order of tasting: Dry>sweet Young>old White>red	Reason: Blending Purchase Comparison	
	Details	*Positive*	*Negative*
Appearance	Level in bottle	Decrease with age	Oxidation, cork
	Clarity	Crystals – sediment	Cloudiness
White	Deeper with age	Pale = new	
	Green	Chablis, Moselle	
	Straw		

	Details	Positive	Negative
	Gold	Sweet? Age 6yrs +	
	Brown tinge	maderized	Oxidized?
Rosé	Bright	Rosé/onion skin	Orange
Red	Purple	Youth in cask?	
	Ruby red	Balance	
	Red tawny edge	Maturing 3–5yrs +	
	Mahogany	Matured 10yrs +	
	Brown	Very old	Oxidized
Depth or tone	Varies	Dense, concentrate	
	Viscosity	Legs or tears	
Smell			
Cleanliness		Wine	Vinegar, pear drops, off!
Maturity	Young	Raw, acidic	
	Mature	Complex, softer	
Fruit	Grape	Muscat, Muller-Thurgau	
	Apple	Riesling, Chenin	
	Grassy	Sauvignon	
	Blackcurrant	Cabernet sauvignon	
	Strawberry – farmyard	Pinot noir	
Depth	Dumb-full	Climate, age	
Taste	Confirms opinion		
Front palate – side	Acid	Freshness	Low bland, high = sour
tip	Sweetness	Luscious	Cloying
Mid palate	Body – alcohol	Extract, glycerine	
	Flavour	Complex, persistent	Simple, one dimensional
Back palate	Tannin	Balance grape/wood	Bitterness, harsh
Finish	Length – balance	Complex, lingering	Short, lacking
Conclusions	Overall		Price

Classification of wines

Designation	Definition	France	Germany	Italy	Spain
Light	8.5–15% alcohol	Vin	Wein	Vino	Vino
Sparkling	Carbon dioxide pressure	Mousseux	Sekt, Schaum-	Spumante	Espumoso
Liqueur	Fortified, + spirit				
Red	Black skin, fermented	Rouge	Rotwein	Rosso	Tinto
Rosé	As red, less contact	Rosé	Weissherbst	Rosato	Rosado
White	Only must fermented	Blanc	Weisswein	Blanco	Blanco
Dry	All sugar fermented	Sec (Brut)	Trocken	Secco	Seco
Medium	Residual sugar	Demi-sec	Halbtrocken	Abbocato	
Sweet	Excess sugar	Doux (moelleux)		Dulce	
Vintage	Wine of 1yr dated				

Legal Classifications

Designation	Definition	France	Germany	Italy	Spain
Table wine	Country, % alcohol, bottler	Vin de Table	Tafelwein	Vino da Tavola	Vino de mesa
Local	+ region or area	Vin de Pays	Landwein	Vino tipico	Vinos de la Tierra
Quality wine, VQPRD or QWPSR	Quality control of area, yield, grapes, alcohol; tasted for area, region, village or vineyard	AOC (AC) VDQS	QbA	DOC	DO
	Higher classification	Cru Grand, premier	Q..Mit Prädikat Oeschle sugar levels approx.	DOCG	DOC
	Riper grapes		Kabinet (73)		
	Late picked!		Spätlese (85)		
	Select bunch		Auslese (90)		
	Select grapes		Beeren- (120)		
	Botrytus cinerea		Trocken- (150)		
	From frozen grapes		Eiswein		
	Greater maturity			Riserva	Reserva (3yrs+) Gran (5yrs+)
Estate bottled	Extra guarantee!	Mise en bouteille au Chateau/ Domaine	Erzeuger Abfüllung	Imottligato nel origine	Engarrafado de origen

Index

accounting documents
    advice note 224
    credit note 227
    debit note 227
    delivery note 224
    despatch note 224
    pay slip 227–8
    sales invoice 225–6
    statement of account 227
apportionment of costs 234
arrivals list 108–9
automated check-in 130
automated check-out 130

bacteria 197–8
bedroom book 121
billing procedures 103
bin cards 239–40
block cleaning 87
budgetary controls 96
building security 75

cancellation procedure 126
catering services sector 5, 9–12
    educational outlets 10–11
    health and welfare outlets 10
    industrial catering 11
    residential outlets 11
central reservation system 124–6
check-in 99–101, 130
check-out 108, 130
cleaning
    disinfecting methods 200–1
    equipment 81–2
    frequencies 83, 85
    materials 79, 200
    tasks 84
commercial sector 5–9
communication
    food preparation and food service
      62–3
    skills 149–51
computerization 124, 129
conference centres 73
contract of booking 134
controlling work 95–6
conventional chart 121–2
cooking processes 42–4
cook-serve 36–7
cook-store-serve 37–9
COSHH 187
customer bills 242–3
customer care programme
    implementation 155–6
    monitoring and evaluation 156–7
customer service standards
    competence 153
    measuring standards 159–63
    operational 153
    setting performance standards
      158–9

dangerous machines 187
Data Protection Act 134, 137–9
debit note 227
delivery note 224
density chart 121, 123
departures list 109
depreciation 231
despatch note 224

direct costs 230
Disability Discrimination Act 136
drive thru 18
duty rotas 95

economic changes 18
EFTPOS 132
electronic keys 131
employment trends 13–15
environmental issues
    air quality and emissions 207
    energy conservation 206
    environmental policy 78
    noise monitoring and limitations
        208
    waste management 205
    water conservation 207
    water quality 207
EPOS 132
European Union (EU) Directives 17,
    20
    Health and Safety 193
evaluating safety 210
external customers 147

fast food outlets 18
Fidelity Bond 140
FIFO 201
Fire Precautions Act 188–9
fire prevention 75
fittings 75
Food and Drugs Act 184
food courts 18
Food Hygiene (General) Regulations
    (1970) 187
    Amendments (1995) 187
food poisoning 196–202
food premises registration 187
food preparation processes 41
    cook-serve 36–7
    cook-store-serve 37–9
food preservation 202
food production plan 47–8
Food Safety Act 186–7
food service preparation 51, 55
food service systems
    counter service 51–2
    ganymede 10
    gueridon 51
    table service 51–2, 56
food spoilage 201
food storage 40–1, 201
forecasting 242–5
function catering 58–62
furniture 74

goods received note 225
guest list 109

HCI 3
HCIMA 13
health and safety
    HACCP 176, 187
    hazards
        controlling 175–6
        identifying 175
        management of 193–5
    policy 173
    risk assessment 177–9
    RIDDOR 179
Health and Safety
    at Work Act 189–91
    Commission 190
    Executive 211
hierarchical structures 94
Hotel and Catering International
        Management Association (HCIMA)
        13
Hotel Proprietors Act 134–5, 183
housekeeper's report 79–80, 111

Immigration (Hotel Records) Order 136
indirect costs 230–1
individual cleaning 87
in-house services 101, 103
Innkeepers Act 134
Innkeepers Right of Lien 134
internal customers 147
ISDN 73

job procedures 94

legislation, food preparation and service
        66
licensing acts 184–5
lighting 76
Local Area Networks (LAN) 129
local trends 19

maintenance
    preventative 77
    regular 77
menu development 44–7
Misrepresentation Act 139
monitoring checklist 88

order form 222–3
order of work cards 95
outside catering 62
overbooking 119–20

payment methods 103–8
personal presentation 148–9
personal service 51–2
petty cash 228–9
Price Marking Orders 184
pricing considerations 235

product knowledge   152
profit and loss   245
purchasing
    function   220
    process   221–2
    security measures   228–9
    specifications   220–1

rack rate   119
rack system   122–3
reception cycle   98
referrals   120
registration   99–101
reservation systems   111–14
room servicing   83
room status report   110
room types   117–18

safety checklist   180–2
Sale of Goods Act   184
security   204
selling price   230, 232–3
selling up   120
sleeper forecast   111
social changes   18
staffing structure
    food and drink service   63–5
    food preparation and cooking   49
    halls of residence   92
    hospital   89
    hotel   92
standard menus   237
standard recipes   237
stock control   238–9

stock list   240–1
stock record card   238
stock rotation   201
storage, cleaning materials and
    equipment   82
storage methods   239
summaries of sales and costs   245
Supply of Goods and Services Act   184

tariff   116–17
team cleaning   87
teamwork   93–4
telecommunications technology   130–1
terms   115, 117
Theft Act   184
Tourism (Sleeping Accommodation) Price
    Display Order   134–5
trade associations   23–4
Trades Description Act   140, 184

units of goods and services   231

Value Added Tax (VAT)   183, 235–7

wastage   233–4
waste management   205
water quality and conservation see
    environmental issues
weights and measures   184–5
Wide Area Networks (WAN)   129
working conditions   20
work schedules   89–91, 94

yield testing   237